Rapid Graphs with Tableau Software

Create Intuitive, Actionable Insights in Just 15 Days

Stephen McDaniel

Co-founder and Principal Analyst
Freakalytics™, LLC
Rapid Analytics to Explore, Understand, Communicate and Act™
http://www.Freakalytics.com/RapidGraphs

Editor: Eileen McDaniel, Ph.D.
Co-founder and Marketing Analytics Consultant
Freakalytics™, LLC

Reviewer: Marc Rueter
Director of Sales Consulting
Tableau Software™

Cover Design: Cristy Miller
Senior Visual Designer
Tableau Software™
Cover Graphs by Stephen McDaniel
*Photo by **Loic Nicolas**, San Francisco, CA*

Rapid Graphs with Tableau Software: Create Intuitive, Actionable Insights in Just 15 Days

Published by:

Freakalytics, LLC
3518 Fremont Ave N # 406
Seattle, WA 98103
http://www.Freakalytics.com

Library of Congress Control Number: In process
ISBN: 1448642507
EAN-13: 9781448642502

About Freakalytics and the author

Freakalytics, LLC was founded by Stephen McDaniel and Eileen McDaniel, Ph.D. Our mission is to cultivate a passion for analytics in our public training, custom training and consulting engagements. Our courses are designed around the principles of rapid analytics. Following these principles will help you explore your data, understand and interpret the data, communicate your findings and take action!

Co-founder Stephen McDaniel has 20 years of experience as a teacher, consultant, leader, innovator and author in the fields of business intelligence, data warehousing and data mining. As co-founder of Freakalytics, LLC and author of "**Rapid Graphs with Tableau Software**" and "**SAS for Dummies**", Stephen is dedicated to helping people understand, present and take action with their data.

Stephen has worked with or been an invited instructor at many leading organizations:

- Netflix
- UC- Berkeley
- Tableau Software
- EBay
- State Farm
- Eli Lilly
- SAS
- The US Department of State
- Best Buy
- American Express
- Yahoo!
- Duke University
- The US Department of the Treasury
- Amgen
- Fidelity Investments
- Target
- Glaxo SmithKline
- Microsoft
- IMS Health
- Oracle
- Pfizer
- Boeing
- Loudcloud
- Brio Software

Our worldwide public training schedule is available at http://www.Freakalytics.com/training and our custom training and consulting information is available at http://www.Freakalytics.com/consulting. You can contact us at Info@Freakalytics.com or by phone at (206) 588-1678.

Page intentionally left blank for proper book pagination.

Acknowledgements

Writing a book is never a simple undertaking. Writing a book to make things easy is even harder as I attempt to identify critical information and convey it in a light, informative manner. I am very grateful to many people for their direct and indirect support in the creation of this book.

Eileen McDaniel, Ph.D. has done an incredible job editing this book. She has gone well beyond the traditional editorial role and mastered Tableau to verify all examples in this book. Her work was critical to achieving a quality publication grammatically and technically.

Marc Rueter at Tableau Software provided a thorough review of the book and his comments, ideas and support were invaluable! His sense of humor and words of encouragement were welcome throughout this project.

Elissa Fink at Tableau Software provided early support for this undertaking and her enthusiasm is contagious! It has been a pleasure to get to know her and I look forward to many more years of mutually beneficial work!

Many others at Tableau provided assistance! I would like to thank Chris Stolte, Jock MacKinley, Christian Chabot and Ellie Fields. A special thank you to the design guru at Tableau, Cristy Miller for the beautiful book cover! Also, to everyone who has ever worked on Tableau, thank you for creating such an inspiring and powerful product! I have been in your shoes and can appreciate the great thought and care that went into creating such a marvelous tool that undoubtedly has delighted many others beyond the author.

I would also like to thank the authors who spurred my interest in data visualization- Edward Tufte and Stephen Few. In my opinion, neither author requires introduction, since they are mandatory reading for anyone who desires to go beyond the basic principles of visualization touched upon in this book.

Finally, I would like to thank friends and colleagues who have provided inspiration and support:

SAS- I-Kong Fu, Chris Hemedinger, Rick Styll, Gail Kramer, Huifang Wang, Rajiv Ramirijan, Tonya Balan, David McNamara, Charlotte Crain and David Duling;

Netflix- Steve McLendon, Brenda Lo, Doug Massey, Lisa Mesh;

Alan Churchill at *Savian Consulting*, Bala Ganesh at *Radaptive*, Rich Brown at *Battelle Research*, Brian Casto at *Group 19*, David Vangeison at *Sopheon*, David Rieder at *NCSU*, Catherine Cameron at *Yahoo!*, Ken Kane at *Insight Consulting*, Brenda Wolfe at *ESRI*, Mike Brand at *REI*, PJ Haselton at *HP*, James White at *NATO*, Michael Berry at *Data Miners*, Jim Esinhart at *Chiltern*, Angela Hall at *Zencos* and Steve Wright at *Quintiles*.

Page intentionally left blank for proper book pagination.

Table of Contents

Page intentionally left blank for proper book pagination.

Chapter 1

Tableau Software – rapid graphs
to explore, understand, communicate and act!

Power, speed, flexibility, simplicity and beauty

These words come to mind when I reflect on Tableau Software. A picture is indeed worth a thousand words, so I will provide many examples to demonstrate why I am so enthusiastic about Tableau. Before diving into the examples, I would like to explain why I decided to write the first book on Tableau.

While there have been many applications over the past two decades that have attempted to simplify data exploration and analysis for a broad audience, only a handful achieved mild success. To be frank, most failed to deliver on this goal. I have personally used many of these products during my career. In fact, I have led software development and product strategy for some of these predecessor products. Unfortunately, many of the designs were based on the underlying technology, hindered by legacy systems, reliant on advanced analytic methods or designed around the technical database architecture. This ultimately led to overly complex products that excluded the vast majority of potential users and were cumbersome even for expert users. Even worse, many of these products actually impeded the ability of experts to easily share and explain findings with the broader audience.

Surprisingly, few applications have focused on how the typical person perceives images and thinks about information. **Tableau has addressed this head-on and changed the landscape forever.** Rooted in sound principles for clear information presentation and good graph design, you can use Tableau to rapidly explore, analyze and understand your data with easy to understand graphs and tables! Based on my experience, Tableau can help anyone who analyzes data in business, government or research to markedly increase their productivity. Even more impressive, people with limited exposure to data analysis can learn and use Tableau to improve their daily decision-making in a relatively short amount of time.

Power, speed, flexibility, simplicity and beauty

This chapter will provide you with explanations and examples around each of these strengths. After reading this chapter, I hope you are inspired to take action and learn how to use this exciting application!

Power

Whether you are exploring your data for new insights, answering specific questions or even deciding what questions to ask, Tableau gives you unprecedented control to investigate, communicate and take action with the information that is hiding in your data! Offering a broad palette of options to graph your data, intuitive means follow your thoughts by rapidly changing your view, powerful functionality to adjust your data metrics for relevant questions and many other capabilities to enable focusing on the relevant data - Tableau has it all. With Tableau, you can work with every major data source- from Excel workbooks to the largest databases. Tableau even enables extracting data from larger sources into a local "extract" file that will accelerate your data exploration and allow offline analysis when you are away from the office!

Profit versus planned profit of major product lines by region (red is below plan and green is above plan)

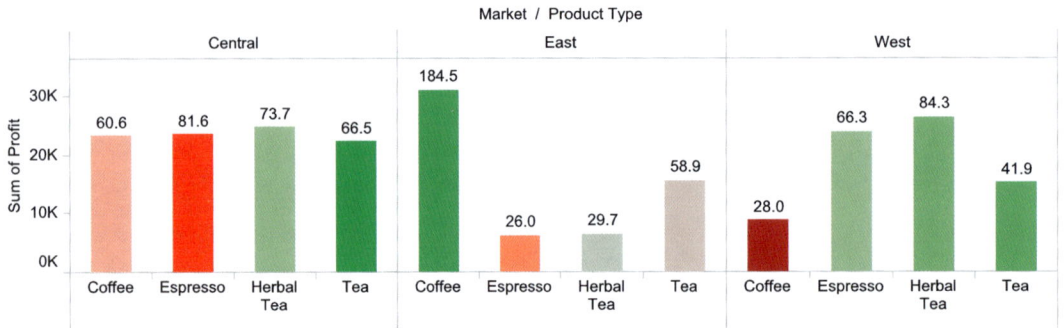

Exploring average time to ship products (size of bubble) by priority (color of bubble) and region against total sales and average profit

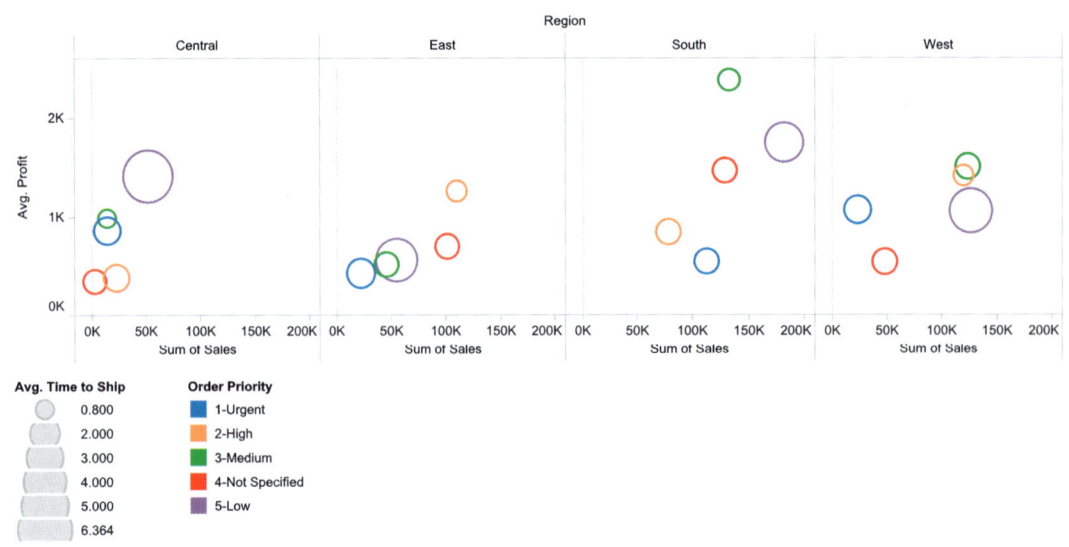

Exploring the relationship of sales and profit across every order

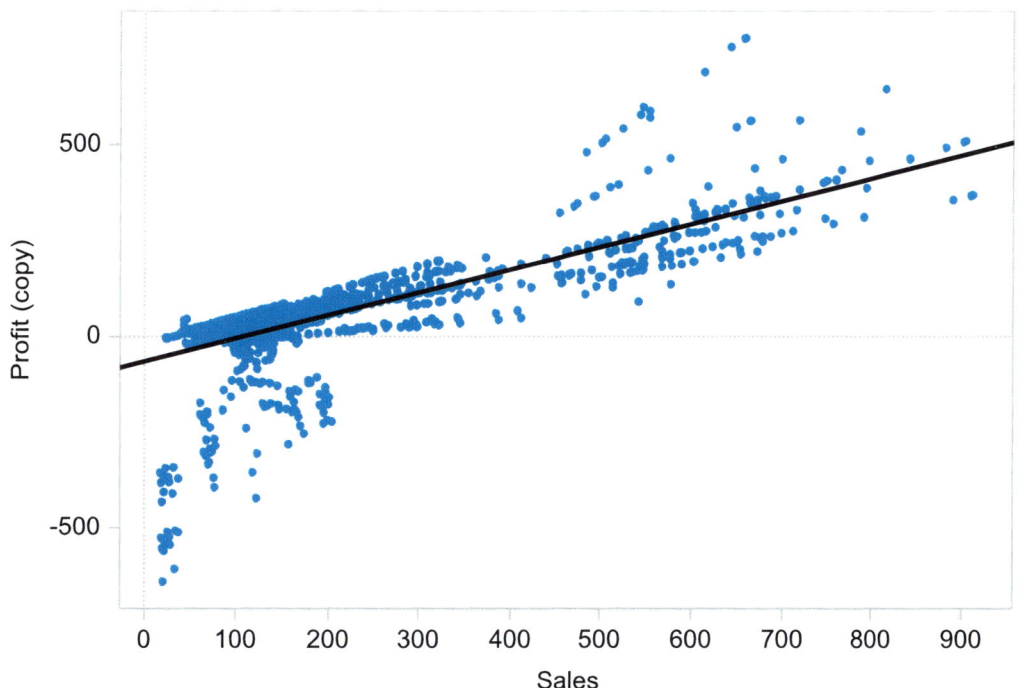

Easily map your data- US government social insurance payout per person (color of square) and payout per person as a percent of amount paid into system (size of square) by state in 2006

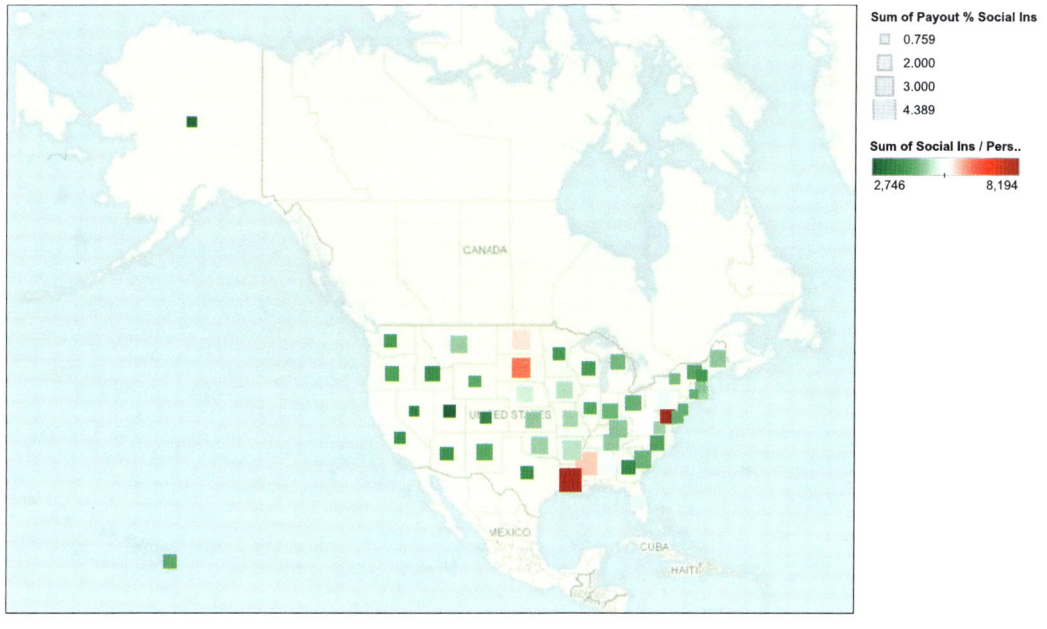

Speed

Faster than you thought possible, you can build presentation quality graphs and tables in Tableau. You can have total control over creating the view or you can ask Tableau to generate the view based on the data that you select. From the view, you can rapidly sort, filter and group the displayed data- with just a few clicks of your mouse. **Each example demonstrates rapid changes made with Tableau in just a few seconds!**

Gross profit data by Zip code – from bar chart to map with one click!

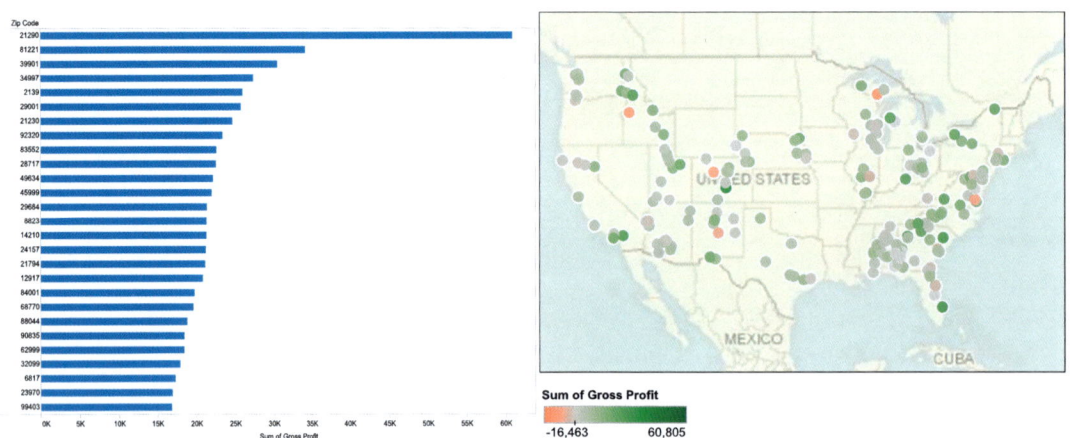

Highlight a data point to examine the underlying data behind that value

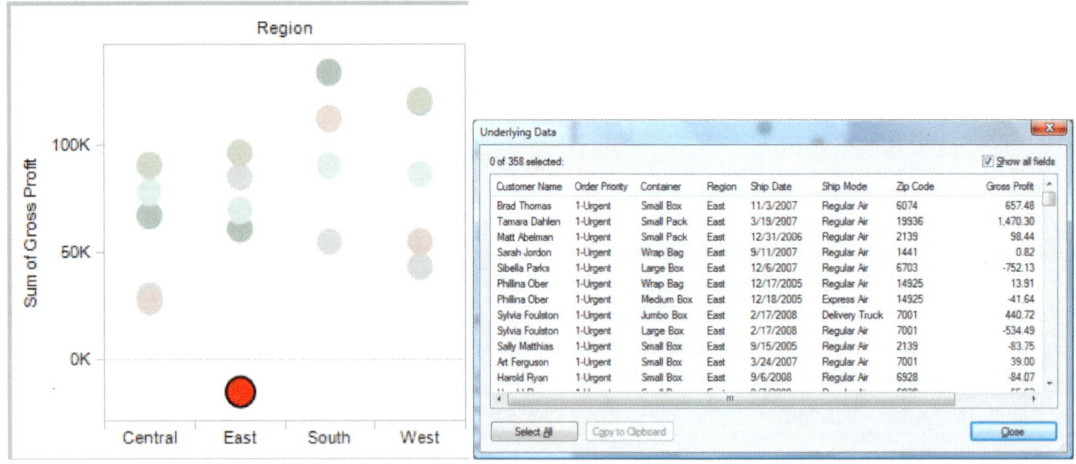

Four views are better than one: From detailed table to color-highlighted table to side-by-side bar chart to color-encoded bar chart in under 30 seconds!

				Date								Sum of Profit vs Plan				
		Sum of Profit														
		2007				2008				2007						
Market	Product	Q1	Q2	Q3	Q4	Q1	Q2	Q3	Q4	Q1	Q2	Q3	Q4	Q1		
Central	Columbian	843	928	915	793	1,271	1,311	1,287	1,177	-237	-252	-255	-267	191		
	Lemon	582	719	677	574	879	1,016	952	854	-198	-181	-193	-176	99		
	Decaf Espre..	950	945	874	840	1,432	1,337	1,235	1,246	-430	-365	-406	-790	52		
	Darjeeling	1,050	1,155	1,220	970	1,583	1,630	1,722	1,439	20	35	70	80	553		
	Chamomile	1,433	1,430	1,515	1,501	2,162	2,023	2,143	2,228	-137	-130	-105	-39	592		
	Earl Grey	991	1,075	1,073	1,070	1,495	1,520	1,518	1,592	81	55	63	180	585		
	Caffe Mocha	1,419	1,512	1,607	1,431	2,138	2,140	2,271	2,124	-511	-528	-583	-1,069	208		
	Decaf Irish C..	908	1,045	1,089	889	1,370	1,476	1,536	1,322	-222	-275	-251	-291	240		
	Mint	399	430	456	375	601	608	643	557	-21	-40	-34	-25	181		
	Amaretto	457	500	556	567	689	705	788	842	-163	-110	-134	-163	69		
	Green Tea	77	87	130	205	117	122	184	305	-13	-3	-10	-5	27		
East	Columbian	2,461	2,940	3,298	2,430	3,714	4,150	4,656	3,607	-89	-110	-142	20	1,164		
	Lemon	580	945	885	823	874	1,337	1,238	1,220	-40	45	55	193	254		
	Decaf Espre..	240	248	257	237	363	351	363	352	-70	-92	-53	-113	53		
	Darjeeling	645	676	710	618	973	957	1,002	919	-195	-184	-210	-182	133		

Profit as a % of Plan — 70% to 153%

	Date							
	2007				2008			
Product Type	Q1	Q2	Q3	Q4	Q1	Q2	Q3	Q4
Coffee	72%	74%	74%	70%	109%	104%	105%	104%
Espresso	79%	80%	79%	73%	119%	113%	112%	109%
Herbal Tea	85%	88%	87%	91%	128%	125%	122%	136%
Tea	95%	97%	96%	103%	143%	137%	136%	153%

Flexibility

You can easily change any part of your view to look exactly how you want, ranging from data point shapes and colors to clear data labels to intuitive color palettes to the way your metrics are calculated and compared. The days of thinking of your graphs as "good enough" are a relic of the past with Tableau!

Create a new grouping of data by interacting with the view in just a few clicks

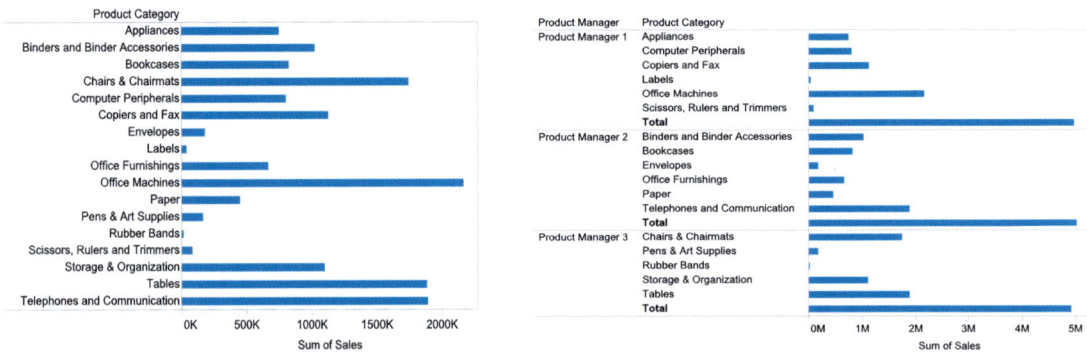

Color code elements of the view for effective communication to your audience

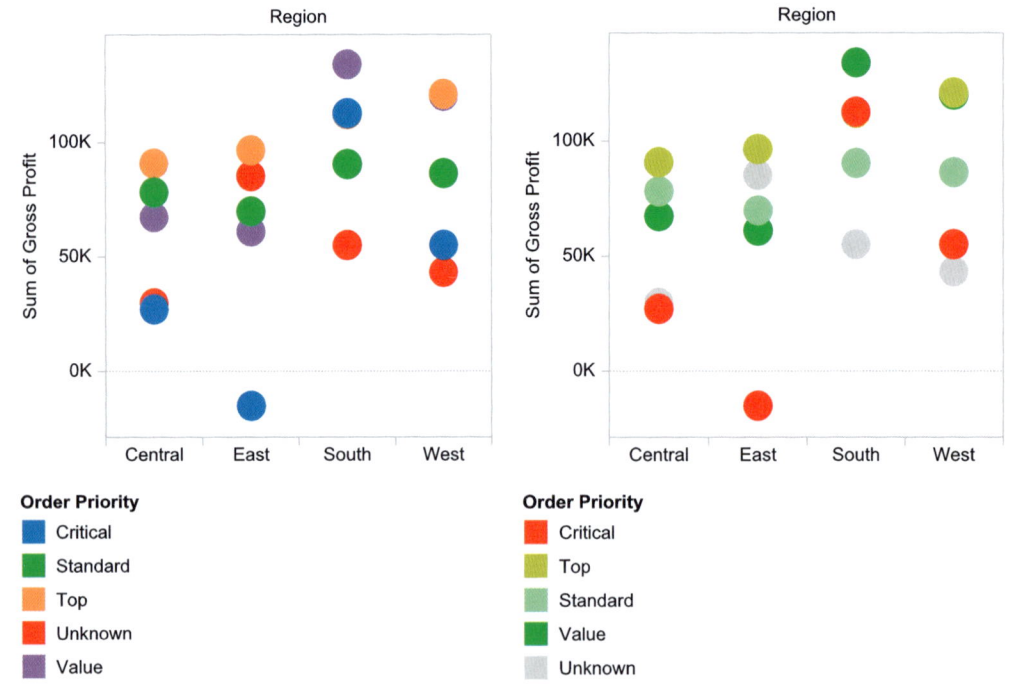

Simplicity

Getting started in Tableau is easy. In the first few weeks, you can learn the basics and begin mastering the techniques of graphical data exploration. Soon you will discover a rich set of powerful functionality to enable rapid completion of more complex visualizations. Those questions that you always wanted to investigate but thought were impossible can be explored with Tableau!

My experience with many other applications is that a typical application requires 2-4 weeks of steady use to learn and remember how to complete several moderately complex tasks. Achieving strong proficiency in many applications often requires months or even years. However, if you work with this book and Tableau steadily over 15 Days, I think you can easily achieve strong proficiency in the first few weeks. At that point, there is still an exciting journey of learning many techniques of graphical data exploration, understanding, and communication. At this point, the possibilities are nearly unlimited, as you will discover that Tableau is extremely intuitive and built to "stay out of your way", so you can focus on your data more than on how to use the tools!

Areas of simplicity
- **Direct interaction with graphs and data items to drag and drop what you want to see**
- **Sort the data automatically or manually directly from the view**
- **Simple and complex grouping of data categories from the view**
- **Easily exclude irrelevant data or include only the items of interest from the view**
- **Wide variety of automated calculations such as *change over prior year* or *year over year growth* without complex formulas**
- **Powerful array of advanced calculations for almost any need**
- **Quickly add subtotals and totals**
- **Readily explore the data underlying part of the view with one click**
- **Shift from other views to maps of the data with one click**
- **Easily export your work to other applications such as PowerPoint and Word**
- **Free Tableau Reader allows interactive functionality for those outside your team**
- **Publish your work to the web for wide consumption of results in your company; no installation of any kind is required for web users to have a rich subset of the desktop application functionality**

<u>Beauty</u>

Create your own works of art while telling the story of your data in Tableau! Combining powerful insights with beautiful views all in one package will keep your audience engaged and informed during presentations. Tableau allows you to explore and understand the hidden value and patterns in your data. Tableau also encourages active use of good design principles, making it easy to impress others with effective, clear communications that lead to lively discussions and actionable results. The live dashboard below is available at http://www.Freakalytics.com/p/4.

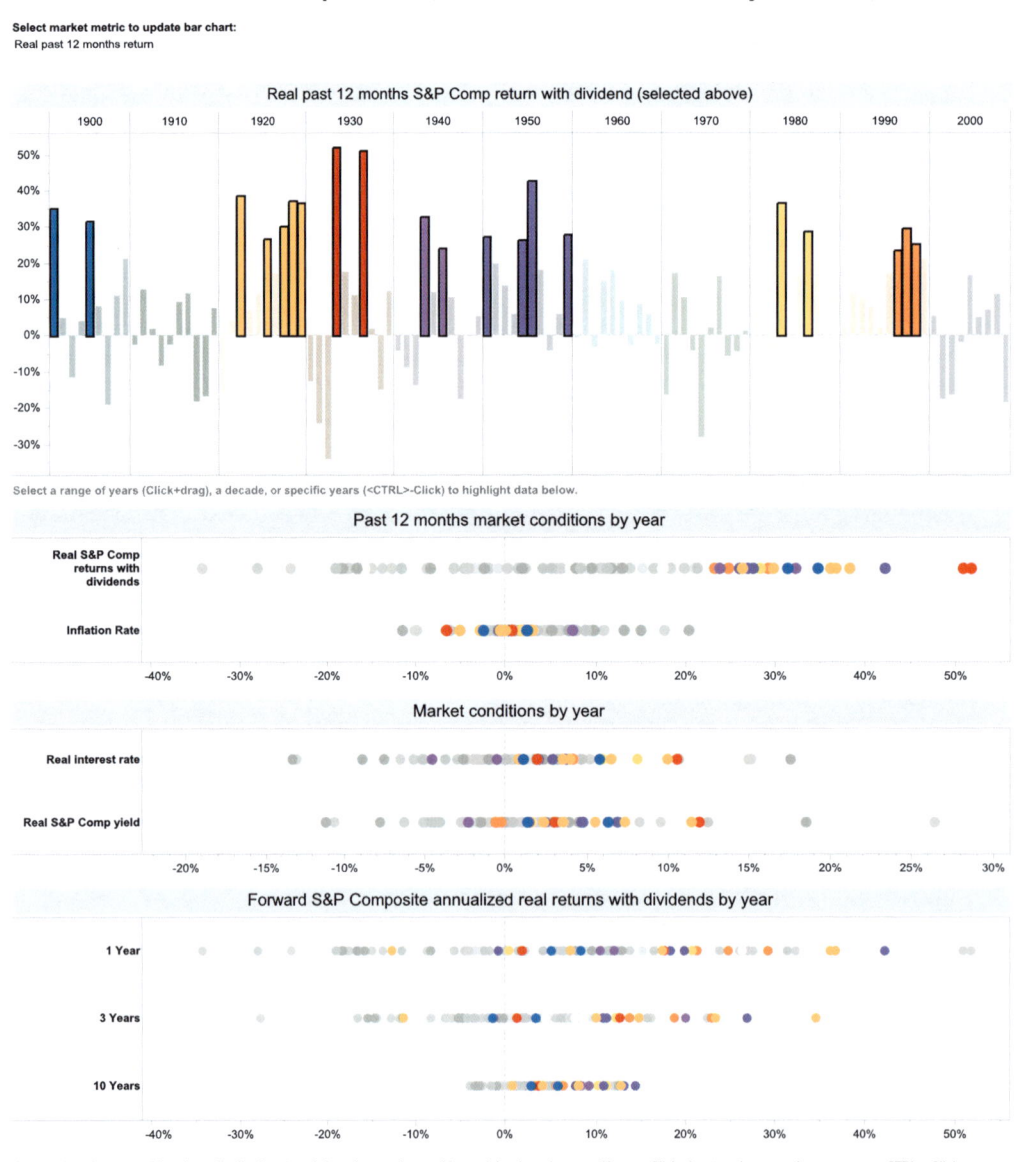

Chapter 2

Build the core: Tableau basics

Chapter Highlights

- Obtaining and setting up Tableau

- Sample data and the Tableau interface

- Your first view of Tableau

- Categorical data never looked so good!

To train for a marathon, you must first walk a mile. The good news is that learning Tableau is much easier than training for a marathon! In this chapter, you will walk through the first "few miles" of Tableau capabilities and even jog through the park a bit.

The first step in learning the basics of Tableau is to become acquainted with the incredibly intuitive application interface. Ironically, one of the greatest challenges as a new user of Tableau is the pleasant surprise at how straightforward it is to use compared to other data visualization applications. Tableau's simplicity and elegance leads you forward with ease while being incredibly flexible and responsive- once you learn the basics.

In the next two chapters, you will cover a broad range of analyses easily available with Tableau. These chapters display a wide array of possibilities while requiring a minimum of detailed application knowledge. At the conclusion of Chapter 3, you should be comfortable enough to begin using Tableau in your work.

Download, install and open Tableau

If you already have Tableau 5 installed on your PC, you can skip this section.

Tableau offers a free software trial if you do not already have the license. The program requires a PC running Windows 2000, XP, or Vista and you must have administrative rights on your computer to install it. Tableau can also be installed on Windows Server 2003 or 2008, which is primarily for corporate use on a shared server.

To download a free trial copy of Tableau Professional, **go to** http://www.Freakalytics.com/RapidGraphs. If you decide to purchase Tableau in the future, you can choose to **work with Freakalytics by registering your interest in Tableau Software with Freakalytics on this page before contacting Tableau**. If you register with Freakalytics before contacting Tableau, **you will be eligible for some great education offers at the conclusion of the sales process** or you can bypass this and go directly to the software download page. If you choose to register with Freakalytics, you will still have full support from the Tableau sales team in addition to receiving great education offers from Freakalytics after your purchase.

Once you register and/or click on the "Download Free Trial" link from this web page, you will be prompted to either Run the Tableau Desktop installation file or Save it to your computer. I recommend you select **Save** instead of Run. If you select to save this file, you will be prompted for a directory location. **Save the install file in a directory that is accessible from a user account on your PC with administrative rights. If you are not logged onto your PC as an administrator, log in as a user with administrative rights. Navigate to the directory where you saved the installation file and start the installer by double-clicking on it.** You will be prompted with the Tableau Setup Welcome dialog.

The Tableau Setup Welcome dialog

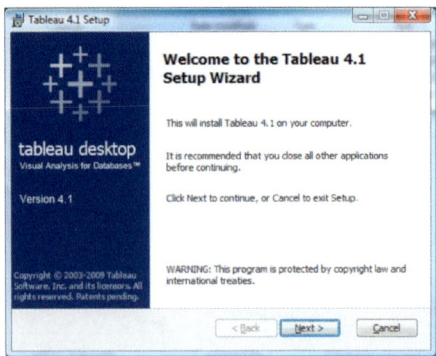

Before you run the Tableau Installer on your computer, **close all other applications**. **You should also pause or disable your anti-virus and spyware prevention software.**

1. **Click Next** on the Welcome Wizard to begin the setup process.

2. The Tableau License Agreement dialog appears. You need to **Accept** the license terms to proceed and then **click Next**.

3. The installer will prompt you to select a Setup Type. Keep the default **Typical** setup selection and **click Next**.

4. At this point, the installer should have all the needed configuration information to begin installation. **Click Install**.

After a few minutes, the installation should be complete and Tableau will automatically start. If you switched accounts to install Tableau, you should log out as administrator and log back in with your regular user account. Then start Tableau from the Start menu of Windows, **Start -> All Programs -> Tableau 5**.

The first time you run Tableau, you will be prompted with the Registration dialog. **Click Register. Enter your personal information and click Register again.**

The Tableau Registration dialog

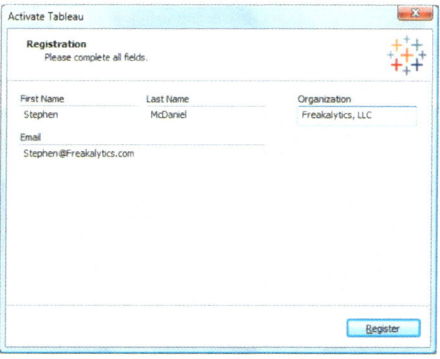

You are now ready to begin using Tableau. *Please note that your free trial will last 14 days from the first date you run the application.* If you experience installation problems, consult the Tableau web site at http://www.tableausoftware.com/community/support

Connect to sample data and review the Tableau interface

Open Tableau from the Start menu of Windows, **Start -> All Programs -> Tableau**.   By default, each time you open Tableau you will see the Start page.

The Tableau Start page

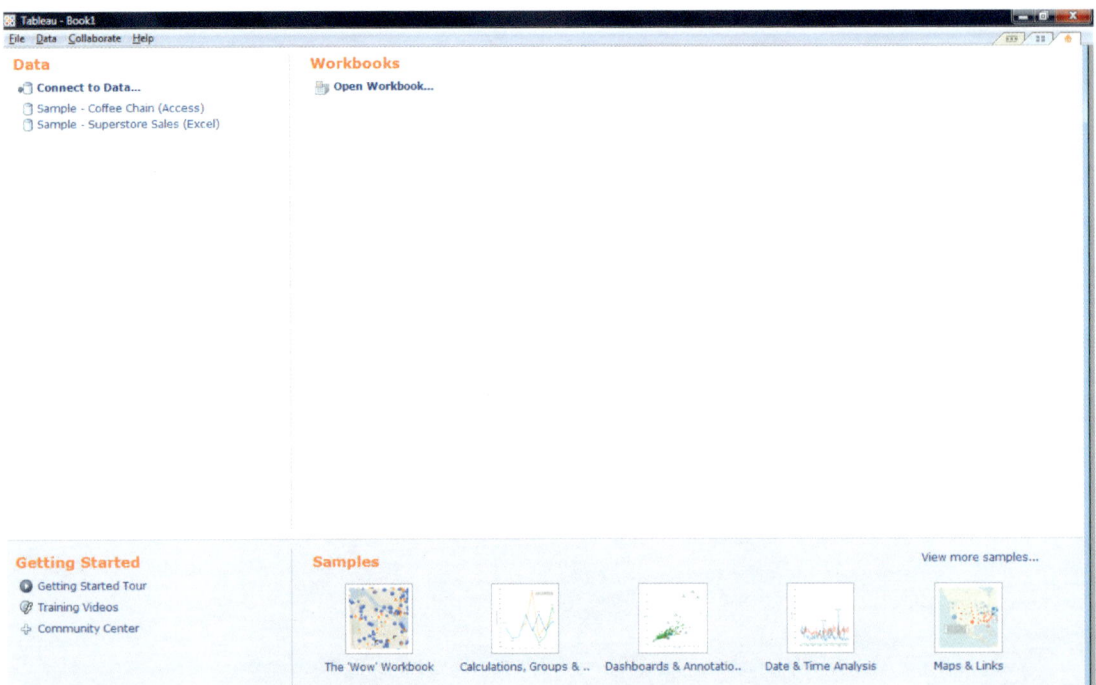

The Start page in Tableau is divided into 4 sections. **Data** organizes data sources, and at this point contains only sample datasets provided by Tableau. The **Workbooks** section usually contains recent workbooks, but is currently empty. **Getting Started** has support links. The **Samples** section has example workbooks provided by Tableau, and if you **click on View more samples** on the right, you can access a large gallery of downloadable workbooks on the web.

In this chapter, you will use a sample data source provided by Tableau, the **Sample Coffee Chain** database. The Sample Coffee Chain is a fictitious national coffee chain. The dataset includes detailed sales, profit, and financial planning data for a 24-month period from January 2007 through December 2008. In the remainder of this chapter, you will answer a number of questions of interest for the management of this company.

Click on the Sample – Coffee Chain (Access) data source from the Start page.   The Tableau Workspace opens with the selected data source available for analysis. By default, the workbook is named Book 1.

! *Alternate Route*: All examples in this book use relational data sources, similar to Excel worksheets, Access tables or an Oracle database table. It is important to note that Tableau behaves differently in various parts of the application when using multi-dimensional data sources or "Cubes" (also called Microsoft Analysis Services, Essbase and other vendor names) as your data source. Although the vast majority of functionality is consistent across all databases, Tableau has specific features that are designed to leverage the benefits of each type of database while working within the constraints of each data source. If you are using one of these less common data sources and encounter different dialogs than those shown, please consult the Tableau Online Help from Help -> Help or by clicking F1.

The Tableau Workspace with key areas highlighted

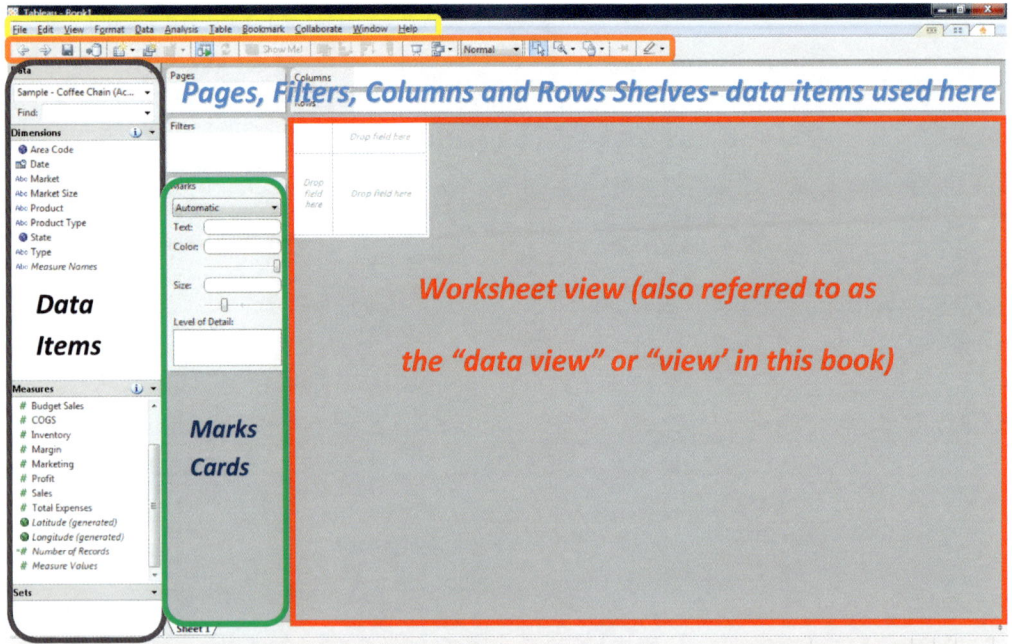

The Tableau Workspace has two standard features common to all Windows applications, the file menu, outlined in yellow above, and a toolbar, outlined in orange. They behave in typical Windows fashion. Specific to Tableau, there are **four key sections** of the interface:

1. **Data Items pane (outlined in black):** shows the data source in use, offers a search box for data items (called Find), and divides the data items available in the data source into "Dimensions" and "Measures". Dimensions can be thought of as data "organizers" or "categories"- examples include location, date, product, and customer identifiers. Measures are measurements or calculations about your data- examples include sales amount, profit, inventory on hand, cost of goods, and number of (data) records. In this book, dimensions and measures in examples are highlighted with green, bold, and italicized text, e.g., *Dimension* or *Measure*.

2. **Marks Card/s (green):** in Tableau, data are displayed by marks, where every mark represents a row or group of rows found in the original data source. These cards allow you to control how the data items are presented in the Worksheet space. For example, for selected marks, you can specify coloring, whether or not to display text, and sizes such as the width of the mark.

3. **Pages/Filters/Columns and Rows Shelves (blue):** where data items of interest are placed to control the data summarized in the Worksheet view.

4. **Worksheet view, data view, or view (red):** where the summarized data are displayed for your review and examination. This is where all of your requests come together.

Show Me Tableau in action!

The CFO of the Sample Coffee Chain is interested in a simple two-year view of sales, profit, and profit versus planned profit by month. She would like this information on one page for her monthly team reviews so she can hand it out without wasting too much paper. Additionally, she wants it to be very easy to contrast the current year with the prior year. In this first example, you will create this view.

1. **While holding down the <Ctrl> key on your keyboard, move your mouse to the Data Items pane and click on** *Date* **in the Dimensions section and** *Sales* **in the Measures section**. The <Ctrl> key allows you to select multiple data items at one time. **Click Show Me!** on the toolbar. The Show Me! dialog will appear with the Line (Discrete) graph type automatically selected by Tableau (if you hover over the icons of the different data views the type will appear). **Click OK**.

The Show Me! dialog automatically picked the Line graph type

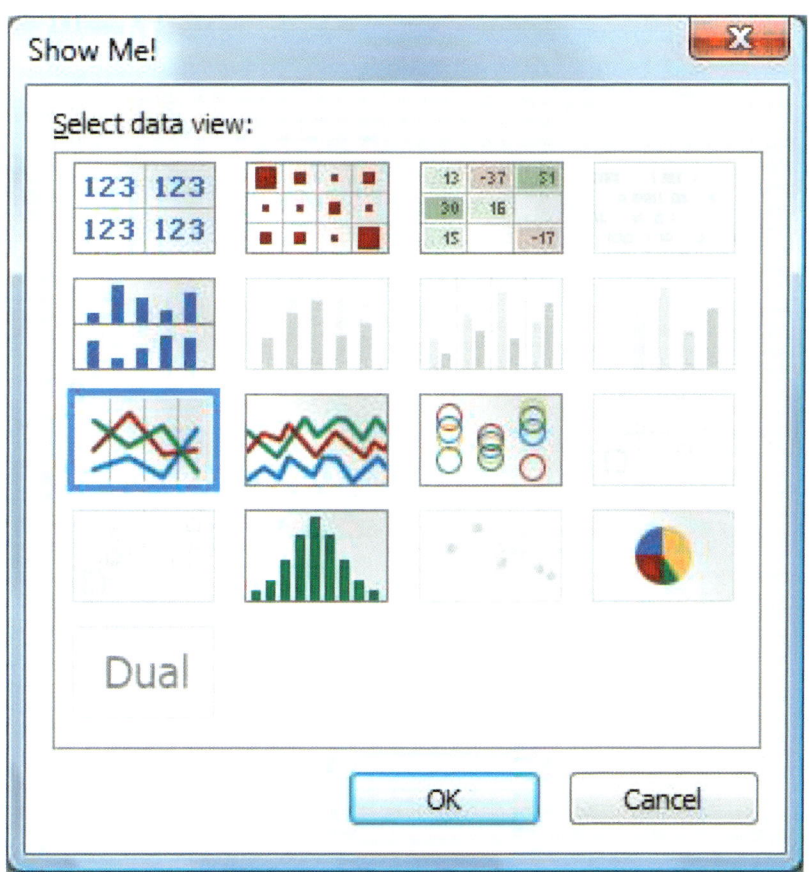

The initial view- *Sales* by *Year*

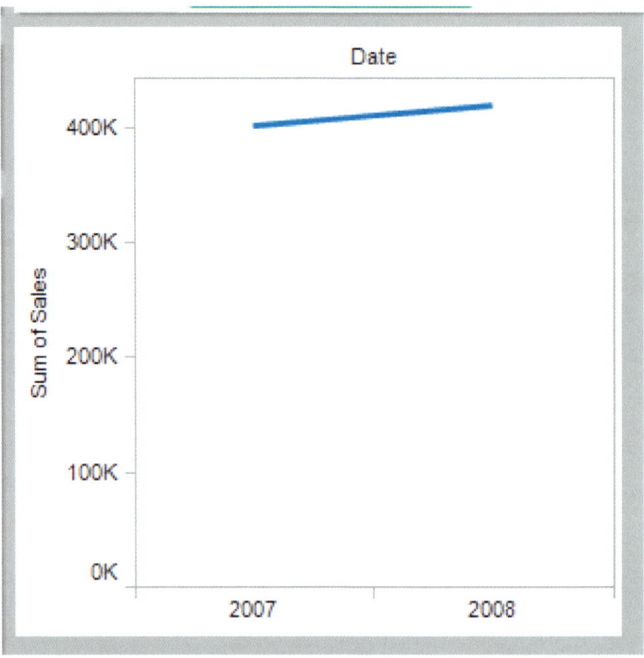

2. Note that even though *Date* is at the month level in the dataset, the data view automatically started at the year level.

3. In data analysis software, to "drill down" means to move from a summarized data item to a more detailed view of the item (if more levels of detail exist). Drill down from an annual view to a quarterly and monthly view of the data. You can drill down on dates by **clicking the + (Plus) sign immediately before the *Date* variable in the Columns shelf** (near the center of the Workspace under the toolbar). **Click on the + sign for *Year*.** *Quarter* will appear to the right on the Columns shelf and visually in the Worksheet. **Click on the + sign for *Quarter*.** *Month* also will appear on the shelf and in the Worksheet view.

    ! *Alternate Route*: To drill down, you can hover over the *Date* data labels directly in the view and click on the + sign that appears to the left.

    Use the plus sign on drillable data items to drill down

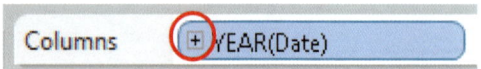

The view after drill-down - *Sales* by *Year*, *Quarter*, and *Month*

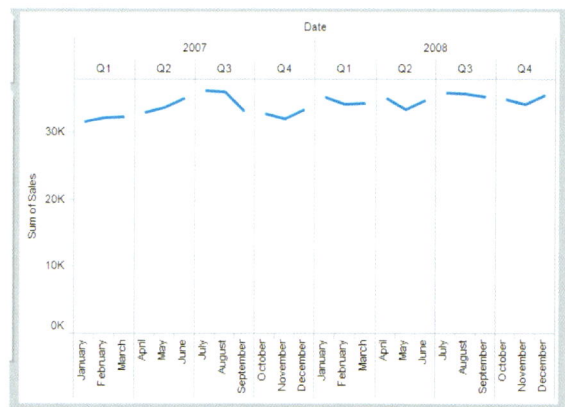

4. Since *Quarter* makes this view busy, remove it. **Click on *Quarter(Date)* in the Columns shelf and without releasing the click, drag *Quarter(Date)* to any spot on the screen except for the view or the Columns or Rows shelves and then release it** (this is called "drag and drop"). Notice how the view dynamically updates with each action.

! *Alternate Route*: You can hover over the *Quarter(Date)* data labels (Q1, Q2, etc.) directly in the view, and when a triangle (the "drag handle") appears to the left, drag and drop it in Data Items pane.

! *Performance Tip*: When you drag and drop, you do not need to drop the item in any specific place – as soon as a little red X appears, when you drop the data item, it will be removed from the view.

5. Since we intend to contrast year over year changes, you can color code the different years by using the *Year* level of the *Date* data item. **Drag and drop *Year*, or the drag handle for *Year* in the view, into the Color shelf on the Marks Card.** Looks good!

The view with *Year* contrasted by color coding

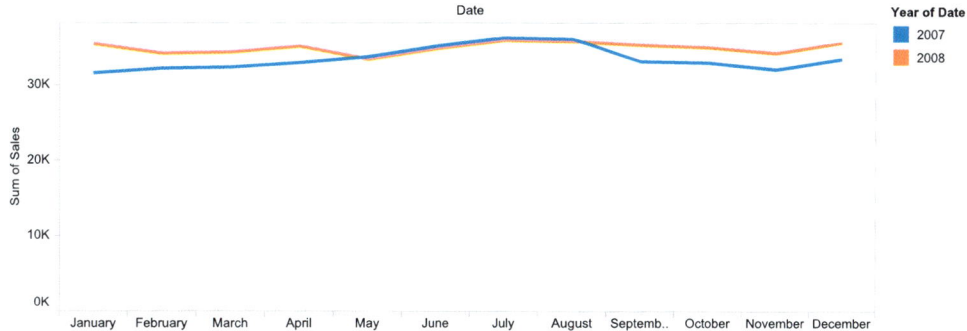

6. **Drag the *Profit* data item to the Rows shelf and drop it after the *Sales* data item.** This demonstrates how any view can be built using drag and drop in place of the Show Me! Button.

7. Finally, notice there is not a data item to compare profit and planned profit. There are *Profit* and *Budget Profit* data items. You can use these two data items to create a calculated data item, *Profit vs. Plan*. **Right-click on *Profit* in the Data Items pane and a context menu appears. Select Create Calculated Field from the menu**. The Calculated Field dialog appears.

The Calculated Field dialog

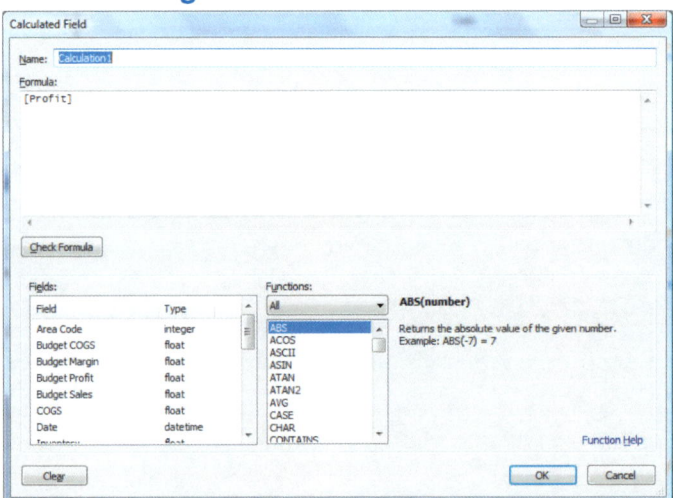

8. In the Formula pane of the Calculated Field, the data item *Profit* is preselected for the formula. After [Profit], **add a – (minus) sign and then double-click on *Budget Profit***. The formula should now read, "[Profit] - [Budget Profit]". In the **Name section at the top of the dialog, change the name to "Profit vs. Plan". Click OK**. The new calculated field appears in the Measures section of the Data Items pane.

9. **Add the calculated data item *Profit vs. Plan* to the Rows shelf after the *Profit* data item**. The worksheet is now complete!

A very informative view:

- The "Sum of Sales" graph shows that sales are barely higher in 2008 than in 2007, with the summer being flat year over year.

- However, if you look at the "Sum of Profit" graph, 2008 has much higher profit levels than 2007. Apparently, in 2008, the company either controlled expenses better or increased prices or sales volume enough to boost profits 40-50%.

- Finally, the "Sum of Profit vs. Plan" graph suggests that the company has some quirks in budget planning because the projected profits were inaccurate. There is usually a difference between actual and planned profits (except in October 2008). The good news is that the company is significantly above planned 2008 profits, a welcome improvement from 2007 where it was always below planned profits. Unfortunately, a spike in profitability was planned for both years, something that should be adjusted or removed in the plan for 2009.

The analysis requested by Sample Coffee Chain's CFO

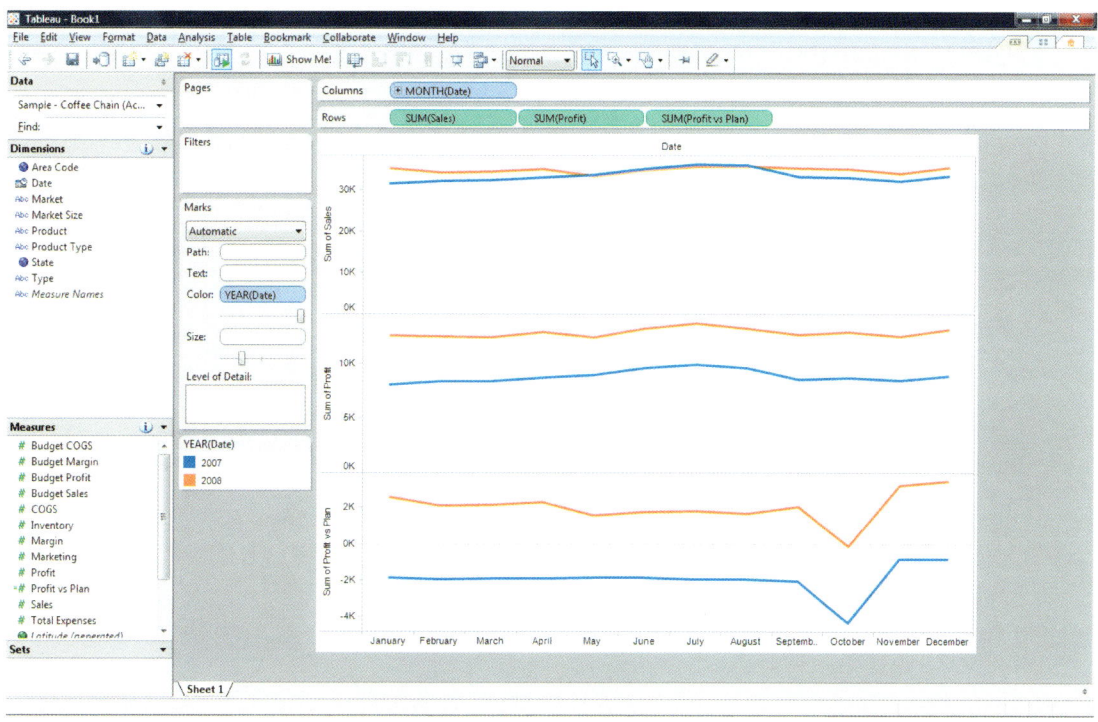

To make it easy for the CFO to use this analysis, you have four options. The CFO could use Tableau (the best choice!) or the free Tableau Reader downloadable from the Tableau website. You could export the view to a PDF by **selecting the File -> Publish as PDF menu item.** You could also copy the view as an image, by **right-clicking on the Worksheet view and selecting Copy Image.** If you want the view in PowerPoint, the Copy Image feature is the best route. When you select this option, you will be prompted for details about what parts of the view to export and details about legend usage in the copied image.

Categorically clear views

The regional sales managers of Sample Coffee Chain are interested in an analysis of profit by product. They will use these data to discuss growth opportunities for new products and possible pricing changes or product cancellation ideas. Here you will create a simple view to show profitability by product.

1. **Click on the Edit menu and select New Worksheet**. A new worksheet is added to the project, named Sheet 2 by default.

2. **While holding down the <Ctrl> key on your keyboard, move your mouse to the Data Items pane and click on *Product* in the Dimensions section and *Profit* in the Measures section. Click Show Me!** on the toolbar. The Show Me! dialog will appear with the Aligned Bar graph type automatically selected by Tableau. **Click OK.** A bar chart with profit by product is generated in the Worksheet view.

3. To highlight the highest profit products, sort the bars by profit. If you hover with your mouse over the *Product* oval on the Columns Shelf, a down caret appears. **Click on the down caret and select Sort from the drop down context menu.** The Sort dialog opens.

The down caret for accessing the context menu

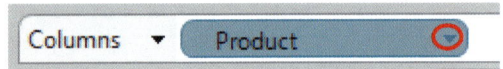

The context menu available from dimensions placed on the shelf

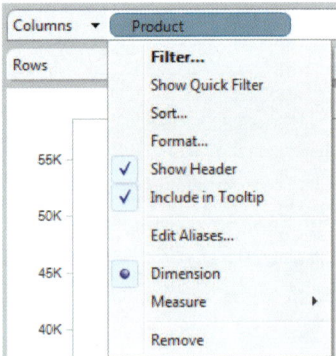

4. The Sort dialog has the default settings of Sort Order: Ascending for Sort by field Data Source Order. **Change the Sort Order to Descending and the Sort by to Field.** *Profit* **is already selected in the drop down. Click OK.** The bar graph is now sorted in descending profit order by each product.

The Sort dialog for *Product*

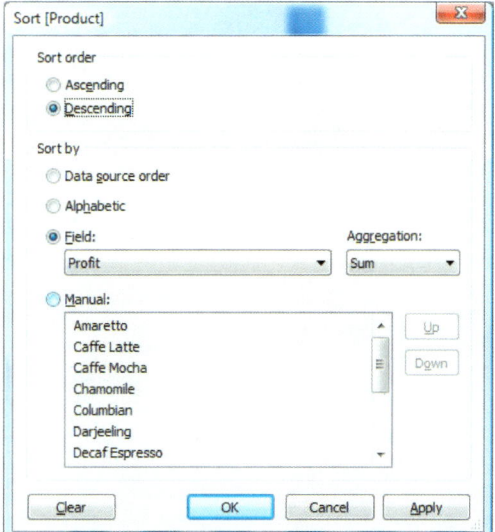

! *Alternate Route*: You'll learn more about sorting your data in Chapter 7, but a quick shortcut to sorting measures that are currently in use is to use the Sort Ascending and Sort Descending buttons on the toolbar, which look like this:

5. Since the regional managers will be interested in the performance of their respective markets, you should add *Market* to the Rows Shelf to the left of the *Profit* data item already in place. **Drag and drop *Market* just to the left of *Profit*.** Tableau indicates where the item will drop by displaying a tiny blue inverted caret behind the *Market* field. Note that the sorting is based on the overall profit across all four regions, not any particular region!

Profit by *Product* and *Market/Region*

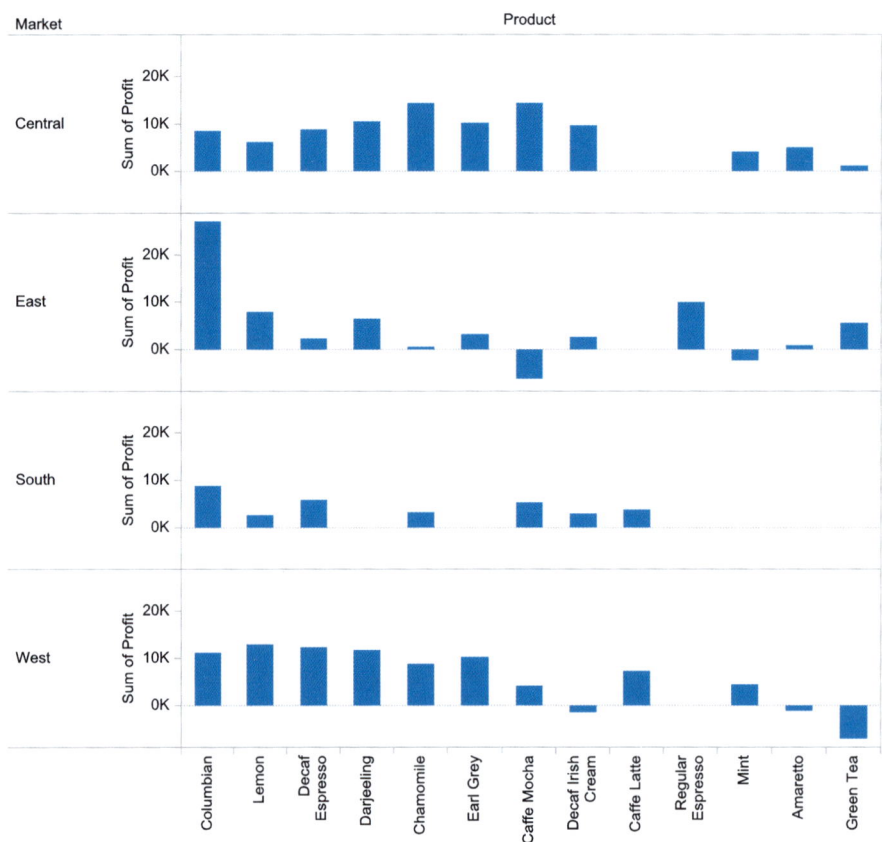

6. To highlight profitability levels, **add *Profit* directly from Data Items to the Color shelf of the Marks Card** (do not drag it from the Rows Shelf because your bar chart with be converted to a table). Tableau automatically uses a red-green contrast to show negative profitability as red and positive profitability as green. Tableau also uses the intensity of the two colors to show lower or higher values. The result is that lower and higher values stand in great contrast.

    ! *Alternate Route*: Drag *Profit* to the center of the view and Tableau will automatically add it to the Color shelf, because dragging a field to the center will "add it" to the sheet using Show Me! Rules.

Profit by *Product* and *Market/Region* with *Profit* color-encoded

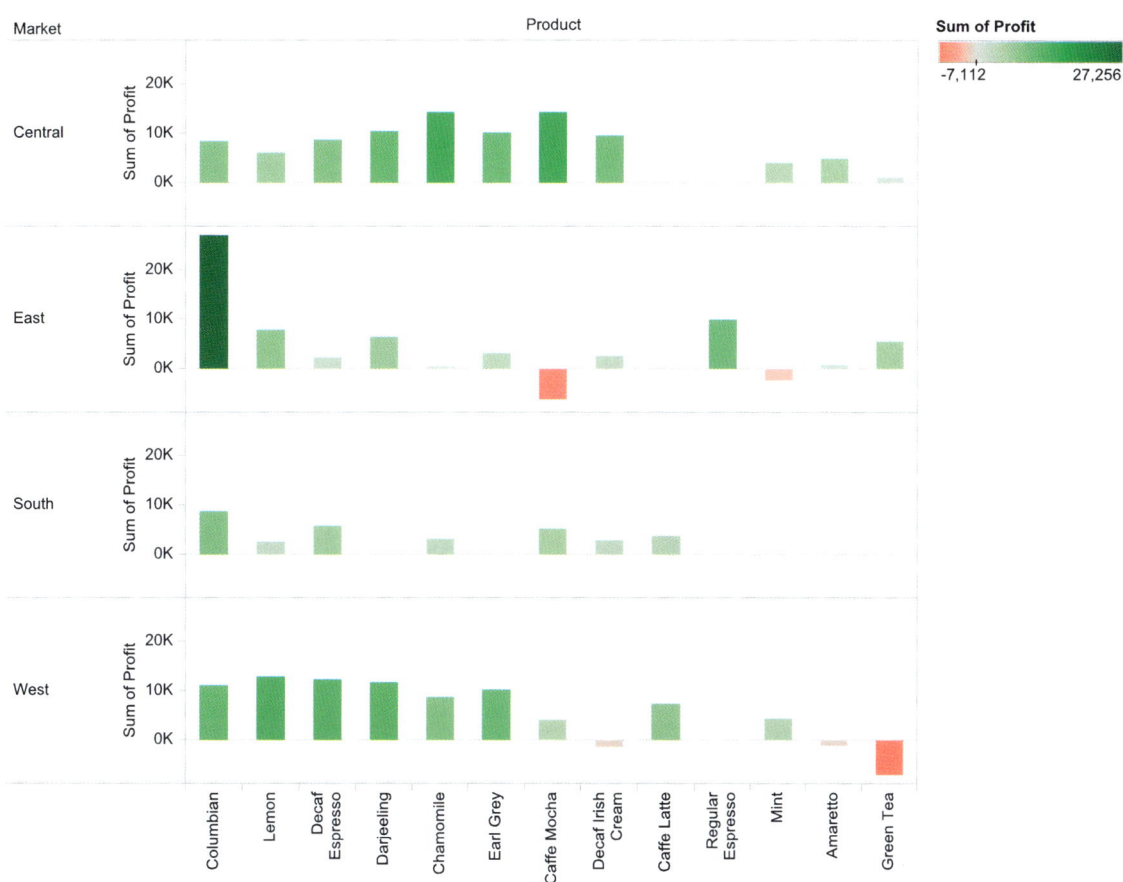

7. Finally, since the regional managers are interested in understanding profitability of various products in their own regions, the distribution shape of each region is informative. However, it is likely even more informative to color encode the value by the profit results versus the planned profit results. Why? This is because pricing may not result in the high profits that are expected for certain products. To enable this view, one simple change is required- **on the Color shelf, replace *Profit* with *Profit vs. Plan***.

Profit by *Product* and *Market/Region* with *Profit vs. Plan* color-encoded

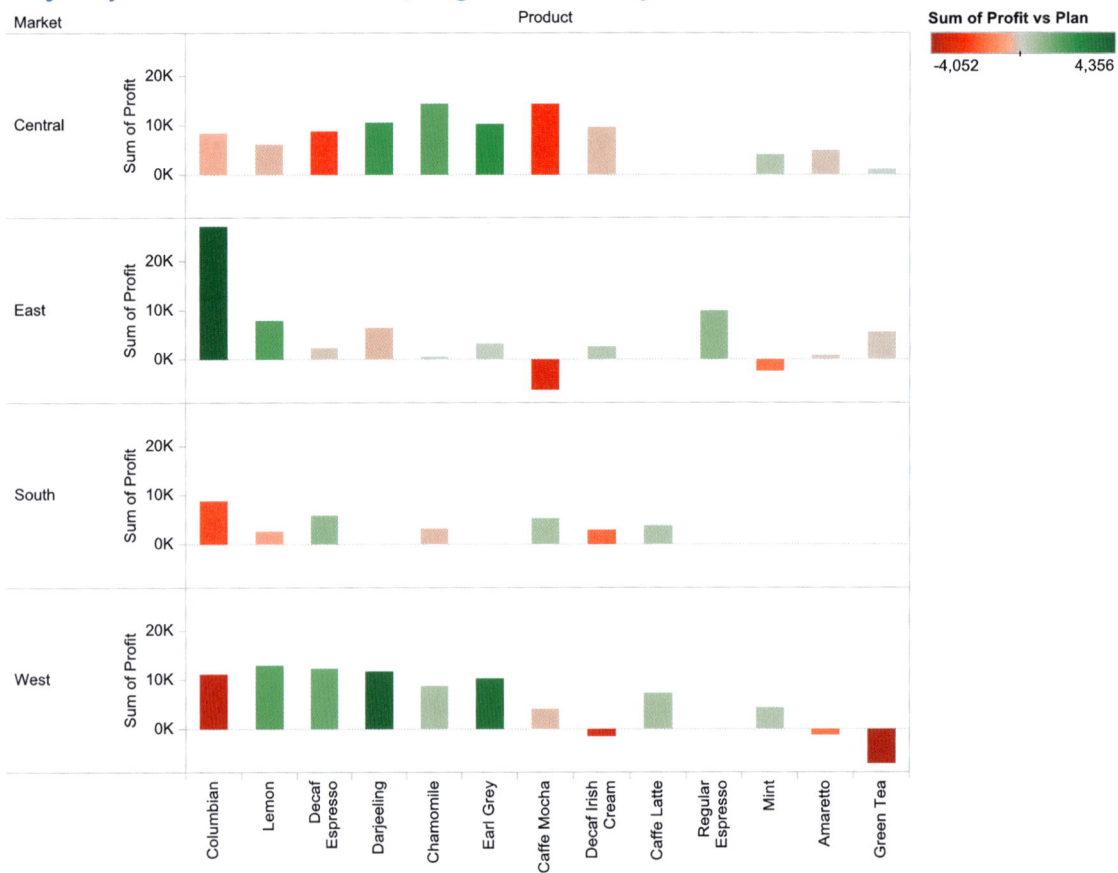

This final view reveals a great amount of information. The overall shape of profitability varies across the four regions with no clear pattern. Additionally, some of the highest and lowest profit items in the regions are often the worst performing products relative to plan (for instance, Café Mocha in the Central Region). This information would likely lead to widely varying regional opinions about future product directions. This might inform the team that product line strategy should be managed at the regional level.

Chapter 3

Go with the flow: more Tableau basics

Chapter Highlights

- Table the data for an in-depth view

- Maps and geographical results

- View shifting with histograms and bins

- Sharing the insights created in Tableau

Now that you have performed some analysis with Tableau and are familiar with the feel and general workflow, you are ready to review more of the application. The regional sales managers and product planners have seen your initial results and they are excited and ready to pepper you with more questions.

In this chapter, you will create advanced tables, insightful maps, and transform histograms into advanced bar charts to get your point across to your audience. The chapter concludes with a brief overview of the many ways that you can deliver your Tableau findings to your team, customers, and external parties.

When tables trump graphs

After the regional sales managers reviewed your analysis of profit by product, the West sales manager called and asked for more details. He said that his area managers could not agree on the weak and strong products and they were interested in whether the differences might be understood by examining product profit by small versus major markets. To examine the details, you will use a "heat map" color-coded data table. Heat map color-coding uses color to represent or highlight the values or intensities of variables so that minimum and maximum values stand out.

1. **On the Start menu, open the Sample-Coffee Chain (Access) data source again. Click on the Edit menu and select New Worksheet**. A new worksheet is added to the project, named Sheet 3 by default.

2. **While holding down the <Ctrl> key on your keyboard, move your mouse to Data Items and click on *Date*, *Market Size* and *Product* in the Dimensions area and *Profit* in the Measures area. Click Show Me!** on the toolbar. The Show Me! dialog will appear with the Line (Discrete) graph type automatically selected by Tableau. **Change the data view to Text Table (Cross Tab) in the upper left corner and click OK**. A Text Table will appear in the Worksheet view.

Profit by *Market Size* by *Year*

	Product / Date														
	Amaretto		Caffe Latte		Caffe Mocha		Chamomile		Columbian		Darjeeling		Decaf Espresso	
Market Size	2007	2008	2007	2008	2007	2008	2007	2008	2007	2008	2007	2008	2007	2008
Major Market	746	1,203	2,384	3,470	4,005	5,684	4,531	6,732	17,996	26,065	5,437	7,779	6,870	9,938
Small Market	1,237	1,704	2,252	3,269	3,196	4,793	6,562	9,406	4,781	6,962	6,407	9,430	5,155	7,539

3. Since we are examining the West region only, **drag *Market* from the Dimensions area of the Data Items and drop it on the Filters shelf**. The Filter dialog will appear. **Click on "West" and click OK**.

   ! *Performance Tip*: If you are working with a large or slow database, filter the data before you add any items to the view (after Step 1 in this section).

4. Since we are particularly interested in the products with negative profit, color encode the profit data by **dragging *Profit* from the Measures area of the Data Items to the Color shelf of the Marks Card.**

   a. By default, a measure with negative and positive values will encode the negative values as red and the positive values as green.

   b. The color encoding is coloring only the text of the profit values, not the background of the cells. To amplify the highlighting of the profit values, add some color encoding of the cells, **Click on Show Me! and change the graph type to "Highlight Table" and click OK.**

   ### *Profit* by *Market Size* and *Year* With Color Highlighting (West Markets only)

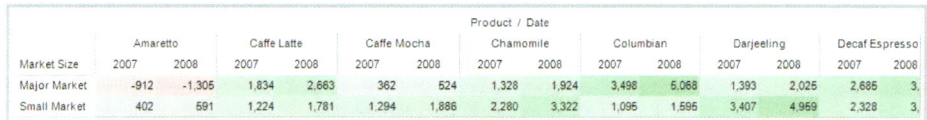

Product / Date															
	Amaretto		Caffe Latte		Caffe Mocha		Chamomile		Columbian		Darjeeling		Decaf Espresso	
Market Size	2007	2008	2007	2008	2007	2008	2007	2008	2007	2008	2007	2008	2007	2008
Major Market	-912	-1,305	1,834	2,663	362	524	1,328	1,924	3,498	5,068	1,393	2,025	2,685	3,
Small Market	402	591	1,224	1,781	1,294	1,886	2,280	3,322	1,095	1,595	3,407	4,959	2,328	3,

5. Drill down on the *Date* data item by **clicking on the + sign to the left of the word *Year*.** *Quarter(Date)* appears next to the *Year(Date)* data item. You can find the rest of the table by **clicking on the scroll bar along the bottom of the table.**

6. To enable easier comparison of year over year changes in profit by quarter, move quarters to the rows side of the Text Table by **dragging the *Quarter* data item from the Columns shelf and dropping it on the Rows shelf next to *Market Size*.**

7. To summarize the profit across both market sizes for each year, turn on the column totals. **Click on Table from the main menu and choose "Column Grand Totals".**

8. To emphasize not just profit level, but growth or reduction in profit year over year, change the color-coding to year over year growth rate in profit. **On the Marks Card, click on the down caret that appears when you hover over the Color box labeled "SUM(Profit)".** A context menu appears. **Scroll to Quick Table Calculation** at the bottom of the menu and a submenu appears- **click on Year over Year Growth.**

Context Menu and Submenu for *Profit* Color Coding

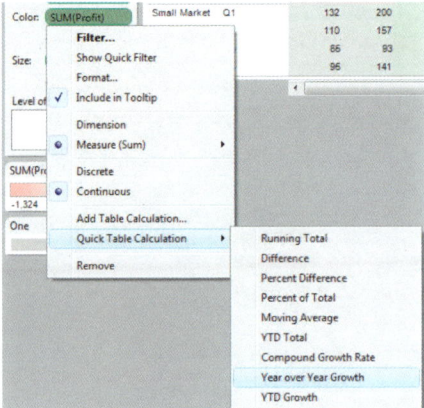

Profit by *Market Size* for West Markets Divided by *Year* and *Quarter*, Color Highlighting by Year over Year Growth

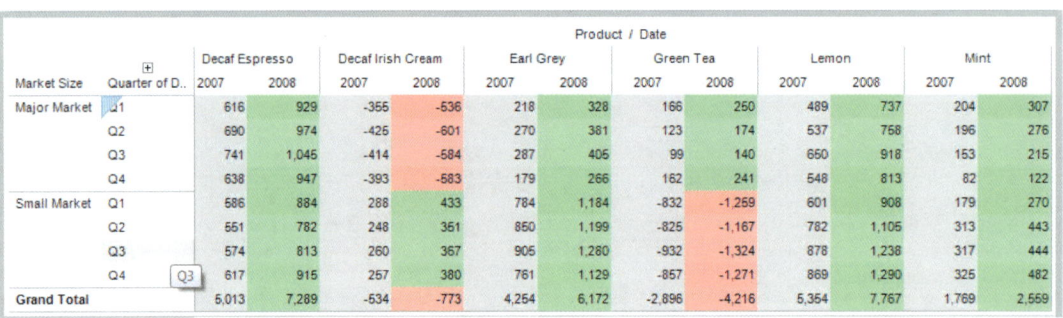

- Since the light red cells are negative profit growth quarters (year over year), a quick review of this table highlights the fact that unprofitable market sizes in 2007 have become even more unprofitable in 2008, a troubling trend.

- Likewise, market sizes that were profitable in 2007 are even more profitable in 2008, a good trend.

- The table highlights that unprofitable products overall are always profitable in at least one of the two overall market sizes. This is a bit surprising and perhaps indicative of the need for further research and possible modification needed in market-based offering decisions.

! *Performance Tip:* The Marks card, which you used in this example, is a very powerful tool that you can use to quickly alter the appearance of the items in your view. It is covered in detail in Chapter 6.

Insightful maps

After the regional sales managers reviewed your analysis of profit by product, they scheduled a follow-up meeting and asked for a map to distribute to the state managers. The CEO's request: "Maps are all the rage on the web. We want to distribute the state-by-state results on a map that is simple to understand. Show us how well each manager adjusted their profitability plans after an abysmal job planning profitability in 2007!"

To meet this specific request, you will use a "Map" view with color-coded values for profit versus plan.

1. On the keyboard, **select <Ctrl> and M at the same time to add a New Worksheet (abbreviated <Ctrl>-M from now on)**. It is named Sheet 4 by default.

2. **While holding down the <Ctrl> key on your keyboard, move your mouse to Data Items and click on *Date* and *State* in the Dimensions area and *Profit* in the Measures area. Click Show Me!** on the toolbar. The Show Me! dialog will appear with the Map graph type automatically selected by Tableau. **Click OK**. A map of *Profit* (shown by the size of the bubbles or "size-encoded") by *State* and *Year* will appear.

! *Performance Tip*: Note that if you are offline, a dialog box will pop up saying that you cannot load the online map. **Click OK and select Data-> Background Maps-> Offline.**

Profit by *State* and *Year*, *Profit* is Size-Encoded (i.e., shown by bubble size)

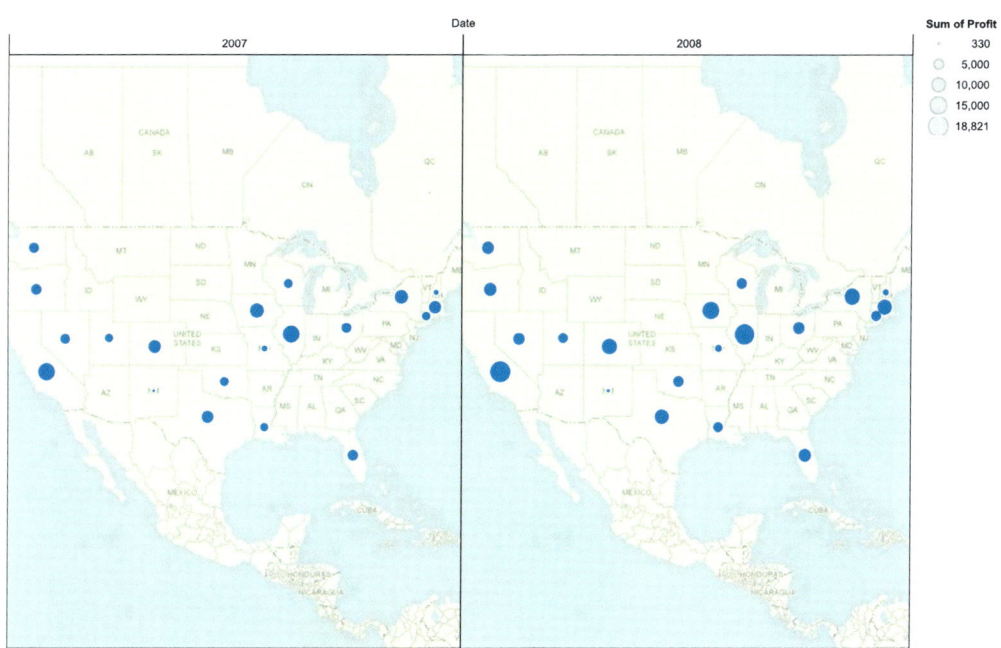

! *Alternate Route*: After Step 1 in this section, **double-click on *State, Date* and *Profit*.**

3. Due to the orientation of the map for each year, you should move the *Year(Date)* data item from the Columns Shelf to the Rows Shelf. **Drag *Year(Date)* on the columns shelf and drop it on the Rows Shelf to the left of the *Latitude (Generated)* data item.** The map view updates with the 2007 map placed above the 2008 map.

4. You should now have the states with the biggest profits already displayed. It will be useful to highlight their performance by comparing them with planned profits. To add *Profit vs. Plan* to the view, **drag and drop *Profit vs. Plan* from Data Items to the Color shelf in the Marks Card.**

5. The bubbles for each state are now color-encoded based on the size of the difference in dollars of profit versus planned profit (or how off the plans were!). The sizes of the bubbles did not change (they still represent profit only). Deep red is very bad (the planned profits were way above the actual profits!), red is bad, gray is neutral (expected), light green is good (exceeded plan), and dark green is very good. Note that this not only makes it easy to see the most profitable states quickly, it also makes finding the states with the worst and best performance relative to plan very easy.

Profit by *State* by *Year*, Color Encoding of *Profit versus Plan*

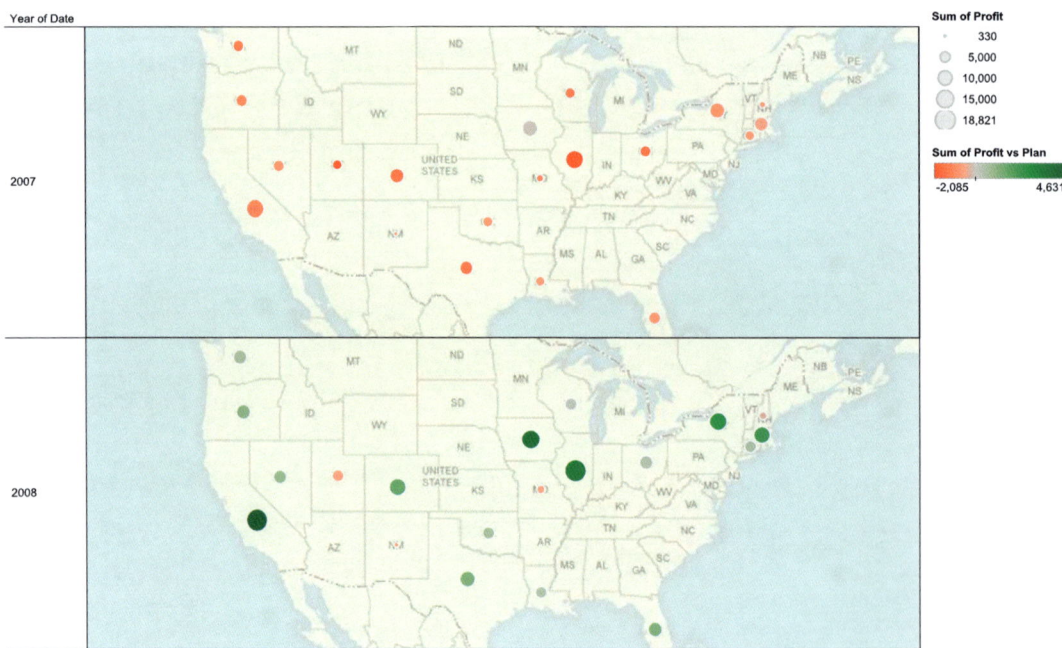

6. Since managers are often very interested in the details of just how far off their plans were from the outcome, you can give them this information in the map as a ratio of profit vs. planned profit. Create a new calculated data item, *Profit as a % of Plan*. **Right-click on** *Profit* **in the Data Items pane.** A context menu appears. **Select Create Calculated Field from the menu**. The Calculated Field dialog appears.

7. In the Formula pane of the Calculated Field, the data item *Profit* is preselected for the formula. **Edit the formula so that it reads:**
   Sum([Profit]) / Sum([Budget Profit])

8. In the **Name section of the dialog, change the name to "Profit as a % of Plan". Click OK**. The new calculated field appears in the Measures part of the Data Items pane.

9. **Add the calculated data item** *Profit as a % of Plan* **to the Text shelf of the Marks Card.**

10. Since you want this metric to be displayed as a percentage, you should format it. **Right-click on** *Profit as a % of Plan* **in the Text shelf of the Marks Card**. A context menu appears. **Select Format from the menu**. The Format pane replaces the Data Items pane on the left side of the Tableau application.

The Format Pane

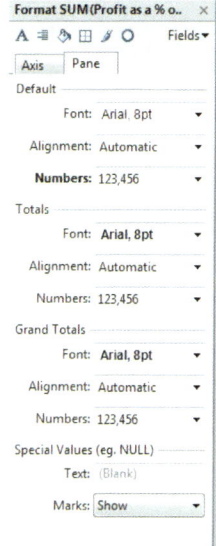

11. **Under the Default heading, click on the dropdown (the down carat) in the Numbers selector.** A dialog appears. **Select Percentage and change the Decimal places setting to "0". To close the Format Pane, click on the "x" in the upper right corner.** The Data Items pane reappears to the left of the final map, which is shown below.

Profit by *State* and *Year*, Color Encoding of *Profit versus Plan*, Text Showing *Profit as a % of Plan*

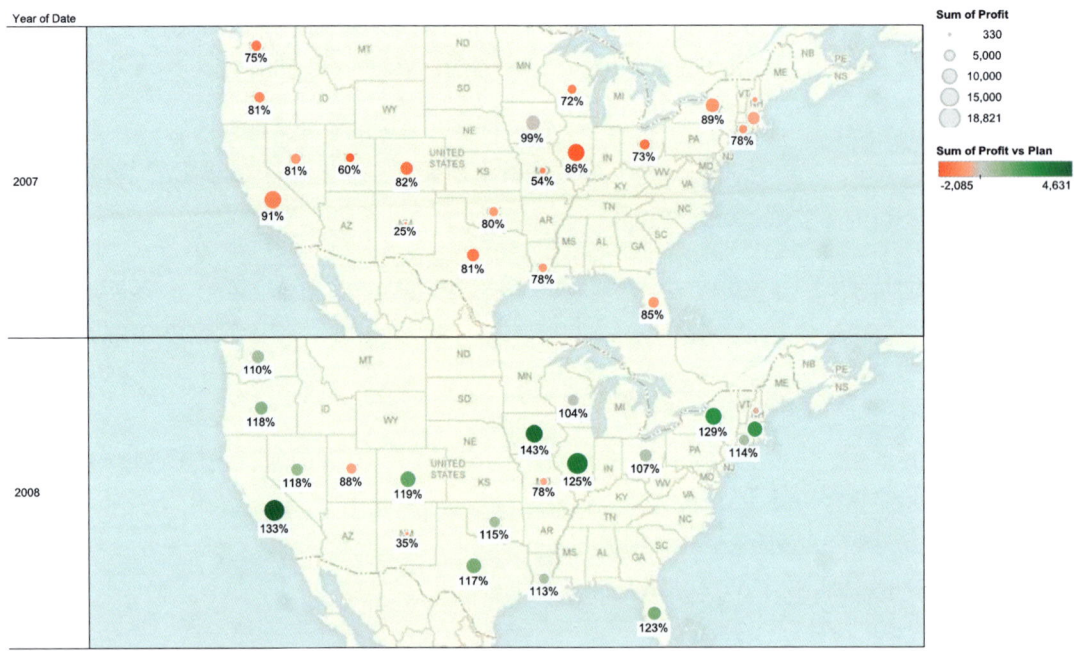

This map communicates a lot of information, thankfully mostly good news! Managers can quickly compare themselves with their peer states and all other states for both years. To easily interpret the features that you added to the map, look at one at a time:

- First, compare bubble sizes between states to see which states are bigger markets. Also, compare bubble sizes in 2007 with those in 2008 to see which states had bigger increases in profitability- for example, California and Illinois were strong profit growth states, which is great, since they also are larger markets.

- Look at the color coding. Notice that in 2007 virtually the entire map is red, so planned profits were more than the actual profits (not good!), while in 2008 almost every state was green (good!). The more intense the red, the more inaccurate the plan, but keep in mind that these represent dollar amounts, so a dark red small bubble may not be as detrimental to the company's overall planned profits as a light red large bubble. Fortunately, the dark red bubbles in 2007 were in smaller markets (smaller bubbles) except for Illinois, which was darker green by 2008.

- The percentages tell you how inaccurate the plans were – the lower the percentage, the worse the performance of the state relative to plan. In addition to quantifying how off the plans were, these are different from just looking at the color coding because they are relative measurements, so you can compare smaller markets with larger markets. New Mexico was way off – profits totaled only 25% of the planned profits but Iowa almost reached the planned profits at 99%. 2008 was a completely new ball game- the vast majority of states met or exceeded their plans! In fact, the most profitable states vastly exceeded their plans by 20-40%.

View shifting- the underrated histogram and flexible bins

One of the product planners came to you and asked if she could give the regional sales managers a better understanding of the importance of lower volume items. She tells you that the bigger volume products often get all the "love" and she wanted to see if her hunch was right, that the lower volume products are more important than commonly given credit.

After thinking about the best way to present this information, you realize an advanced form of a histogram (a bar chart that counts of items divided by category) would offer abundant insight into this question.

To meet this specific request, you will use a "Histogram" view with size- and color-coded values for profit. You will categorize sales into "bins" to create the histogram chart bars.

1. **Use <Ctrl>-M to add a New Worksheet.** It is named Sheet 5 by default.

2. **Click on *Sales* in the Measures area and then click on Show Me!.** The Show Me! dialog will appear with the Aligned Bar graph type automatically selected by Tableau. **Change the view type to Histogram,** which appears as a single bar chart with a central peak toward the bottom center. **Click OK**. A Histogram of *Sales* will appear with number of sales records automatically binned into intervals of 100: 0 to 99 is the 0 bar, 100 to 199 is the 100 bar, and so on.

Sales Histogram- understand the volume of sales transactions by amount

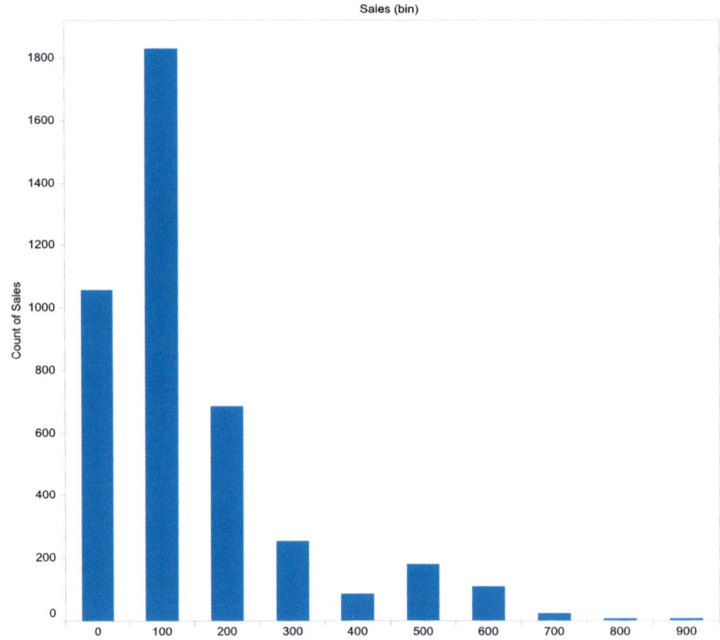

3. Note that with the data used in this sample, a count of sales records in each bin is not very useful. This is a simple summary of the number of monthly sales records for each item in each area code. To make this much more informative, change *CNT (Sales)* to *SUM (Sales)*. **Click on the down caret next to** *CNT (Sales)* **in the Row Shelf, and select Measure (Count) and change the aggregate function to Sum.** The histogram is now considered an aligned bar chart by Tableau, you will see this if you click on Show Me!. Technically, this is no longer a histogram chart since it no longer displays counts, but you have used the histogram as a basis to describe the sales data. As an alternate path, you could have first binned the data and used an aligned bar chart.

4. Next, you want to differentiate between year and region. **Add** *Date* **to the Columns Shelf to the left of the** *Sales (bin)* **item already there and add** *Market* **to the Rows Shelf to the left of the** *Sales* **data item.** Eight charts appear in the view – each of these will be referred to as a pane.

Sales Histogram by *Year* and *Market*

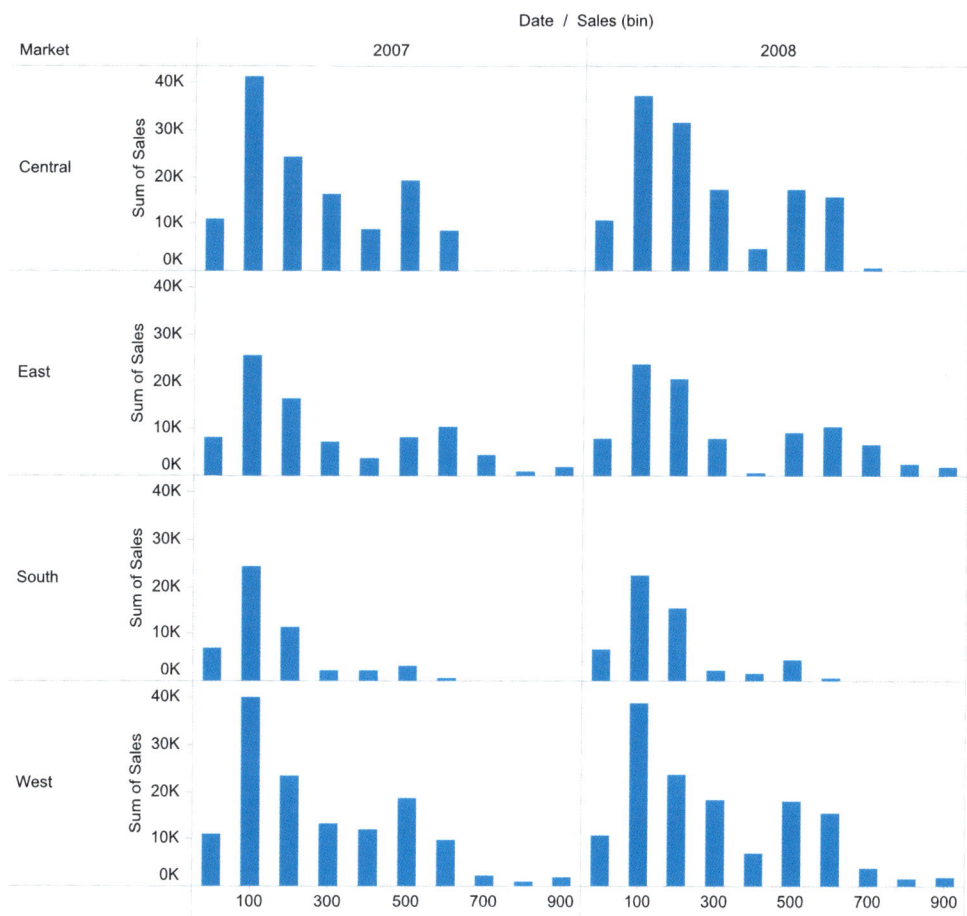

Note the different patterns found in the different regions. West and Central have pronounced peaks at 100 and 500, East and South have less pronounced peaks at 100 and East has more data at the upper end of the binned sales.

Next, you need to add profitability to contrast with sales. This can be accomplished by several simultaneous methods (similar to what you did above on the map): color coding the bars, sizing the bars, and placing profit percentages above each bar.

5. **From the Measures area, add *Profit* three times to the Marks Card: Text, Color, and Size**.

6. You have to fix this up a little- the text is busy and detracts from the key view purpose. To better calculate the profit that is above each sales bin bar so that it is easier to understand, change it from sum of profit to percent of profit for that pane. **Click on the down caret next to *SUM (Profit)* in the Text shelf on the Marks Card and select Add Table Calculation from the dropdown.** The Table Calculation dialog appears.

The Table Calculation dialog

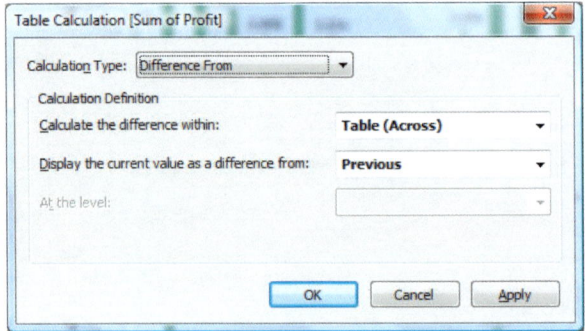

7. In the Table Calculation dialog, **change Calculation Type to Percent of Total, change Compute the Total Within to Pane, and click OK.** The text values change to percentages in each view pane. These percentages are the percent of total profit for that pane in each binned sales bar. You notice that the default format is too precise for this purpose. **Right-click on *SUM (Profit)* in the Text box of the Marks Card, and select Format from the context menu.** The Formats pane replaces the Data Items pane on the left side of the Tableau application. **Click on the dropdown by the Default Numbers selector, a dialog appears, select Percentage and change the Decimal places setting to "0". To close the Format Pane, click on the "x" at the upper right corner.** The Data Items pane reappears to the left of the view.

Sales Binned by *Year* and *Market, Profit* highlighted as percent of pane and encoded by both color and bar size

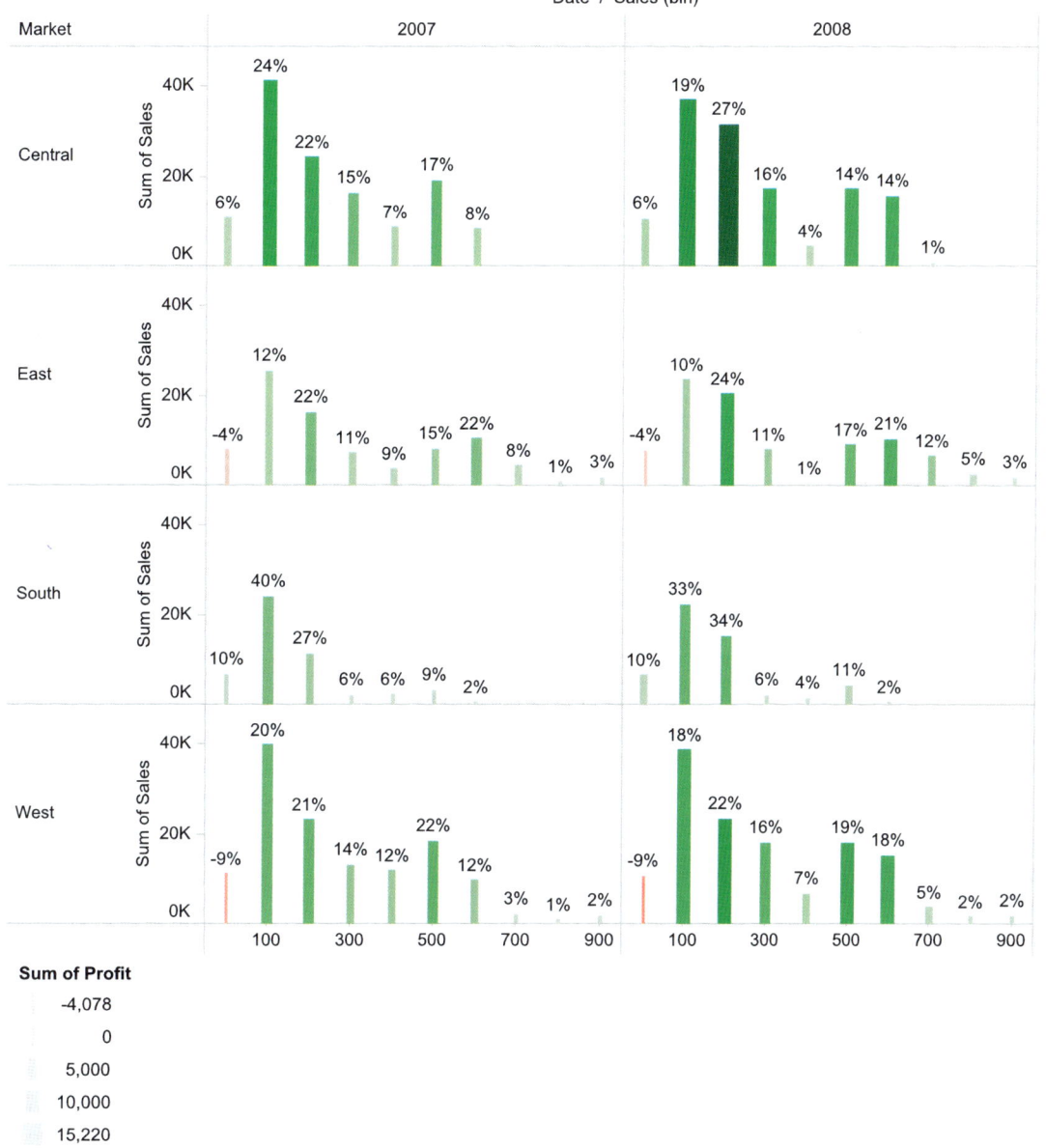

You meet with the product planner to explain this insightful view. Some key insights stand out:

- Examining the binned monthly sales amounts on the horizontal axis, you can see that the highest revenue products are a relatively minor portion of the profits (profit percentage contribution is at top of each bar) across the entire company. For example, the East saw just 4%-8% of all profits generated by products generating revenue of $800-$1,000 per month.

- Examining the annual sales represented by bar heights, you can observe that products with the highest total sales rarely generate the greatest profitability, but they are typically very profitable nonetheless. For example, in the West in 2008, $100 per month products generated the greatest sales, but only 18% of profits, so they were not the highest profit makers in the pane. That would be products in the $200 bin (22%) followed by products in the $500 bin (19%). The South region is the exception: in 2007, the $100 bin generated the most profit (40%), and in 2008, the $100 bin (33%) was essentially tied for the highest profit with the $200 bin (34%).

- The East and West have pronounced profitability at the mid-sales volume product areas, with more than 34% to 40% of all profits being generated by these products, generating sales of $500-$700 per month.

- Another interesting point about this view is that the data in each pane exhibit a primary peak in annual sales at around $100 and a secondary peak at around $500. This is also known as a bimodal distribution.

Exporting results to share your insights

You have several options for distributing your results:

1) Sit down with the recipients and interactively explore the results and data via Tableau.

2) Install a copy of Tableau or a free Tableau Reader (downloadable from the Tableau website) for the recipients and share the Tableau project built through Chapter 2 and 3. Tableau has a server product built to make this sharing centralized and more manageable.

3) Export the results in the Tableau project via the Publish as PDF function, via **File -> Publish as PDF**.

    a. This is a very easy way to transfer Tableau results to people without Tableau.

    b. Unfortunately, unless you have purchased Adobe Acrobat (not just the free Reader version), you will not be able to edit and rearrange the results exported via this method.

4) Individually copy and paste views from Tableau to other applications, such as Microsoft PowerPoint and Word, via **Edit -> Copy -> Copy Image or by right-clicking over the view and selecting Copy Image.**

    a. This is flexible and works across many Windows applications. The image is of high quality for general purpose presentations. I frequently use this method throughout this book.

    b. Unfortunately, if you want to update a slide deck or Word document on a frequent basis, there is no automation method for this task, so you will need to copy it each time from Tableau.

5) Use the "dashboard" functionality in Tableau to combine multiple views created in a Tableau project into one unified "dashboard" view. Access this capability via **Edit -> New Dashboard**.

Page intentionally left blank for proper book pagination.

Chapter 4

Creating and managing Views to explore and inform

Chapter Highlights

- Understanding the core view categories in Tableau

  - Text Tables- when the details are the point

  - Heat Maps- how hot is it?

  - Bar Charts- the most flexible views

Views are the foundation of Tableau, so mastering them is the key to optimizing your visualization insights. In this chapter, you will learn about the core view types.

In Tableau, you can use the "Show Me!" button to display the array of seventeen specific view types. Tableau automatically highlights the view that it "guesses" will be the most useful for the data items that you selected, and lets you know which other views are available. Views that are not appropriate due to the nature of your selected data items are grayed out on the Show Me! dialog.

If you accept the "Show Me!" view, you can easily change the view type later via "Show Me" or by your own manual modifications to the shelves and settings. In fact, when you manually adjust your view, Tableau may surprise you by automatically changing it to the appropriate one - that is the beauty of Tableau!

I have grouped the seventeen templates into eight logical categories for your convenience. In this chapter, the first three view categories are covered. Please note the view templates are addressed in the same order as depicted in the Show Me! dialog box.

Each view category and view type is described along with a simple example and the occasional advanced one. The following table summarizes eight of the seventeen view types and the data items required to use them as the basis of a view.

View Category / Name	View Example	Required Dimension Items	Required Measure Items
Text Table- **Text Table (Cross-Tab)**		1 or more (may be 0 if have at least 1 measure)	1 or more (may be 0 if have at least 1 dimension)
Text Table- **Highlight Table**		1 or more	1 or more
Heat Map- **Heat Map**		1 or more	1 or 2
Bar Chart- **Aligned Bar**		0 or more	1 or more
Bar Chart- **Stacked Bar**		2 or more	1 or more
Bar Chart- **Side-by-Side Bar**		1 or more	2 or more
Bar Chart- **Bar With Measure on Color**		1 or more	2 or more
Bar Chart- **Histogram**		0 or more	1

Text Tables- an eye for detail

A Text Table is commonly referred to as a cross-tab or pivot table. It provides a way to display counts or measures relative to categorical variables. Tables are useful when it is important to look up individual data point values or when you want to compare them across one or more levels of dimensional detail.

1. **Text Table**- best choice when you require the ability to reference specific values for data precision and data checking. It is also the view that many Excel users are the most comfortable using. Text Tables are very flexible in Tableau and can easily morph into other view types, so if you want to review detailed data values before moving on to other view types, they are a good starting point.

! Performance Tip: There is no need to add every field to the text table. Rather, start with a summary containing just a few crucial dimensions and then drill into the interesting areas by filtering and adding more detail when needed.

A Text Table excerpt showing *Profit* and *Profit versus Plan* by *Market, Product, Year* and *Quarter*

													Date	
				Sum of Profit									Sum of Profit vs Plan	
		2007				2008				2007				
Market	Product	Q1	Q2	Q3	Q4	Q1	Q2	Q3	Q4	Q1	Q2	Q3	Q4	Q1
Central	Columbian	843	928	915	793	1,271	1,311	1,287	1,177	-237	-252	-255	-267	191
	Lemon	582	719	677	574	879	1,016	952	854	-198	-181	-193	-176	99
	Decaf Espre..	950	945	874	840	1,432	1,337	1,235	1,246	-430	-365	-406	-790	52
	Darjeeling	1,050	1,155	1,220	970	1,583	1,630	1,722	1,439	20	35	70	80	553
	Chamomile	1,433	1,430	1,515	1,501	2,162	2,023	2,143	2,228	-137	-130	-105	-39	592
	Earl Grey	991	1,075	1,073	1,070	1,495	1,520	1,518	1,592	81	55	63	180	585
	Caffe Mocha	1,419	1,512	1,607	1,431	2,138	2,140	2,271	2,124	-511	-528	-583	-1,069	208
	Decaf Irish C..	908	1,045	1,089	889	1,370	1,476	1,536	1,322	-222	-275	-251	-291	240
	Mint	399	430	456	375	601	608	643	557	-21	-40	-34	-25	181
	Amaretto	457	500	556	567	689	705	788	842	-163	-110	-134	-163	69
	Green Tea	77	87	130	205	117	122	184	305	-13	-3	-10	-5	27
East	Columbian	2,461	2,940	3,298	2,430	3,714	4,150	4,656	3,607	-89	-110	-142	20	1,164
	Lemon	580	945	885	823	874	1,337	1,238	1,220	-40	45	55	193	254
	Decaf Espre..	240	248	257	237	363	351	363	352	-70	-92	-53	-113	53
	Darjeeling	645	676	710	618	973	957	1,002	919	-195	-184	-210	-182	133

A section of the same Text Table color-encoded by *Product Type*

			Date / Date			
			2007			
			Sum of Profit		Sum of Profit vs Plan	
Market	Product Type	Product	Q1	Q2	Q1	Q2
Central	Coffee	Decaf Irish Cream	908	1,045	-222	-275
		Columbian	843	928	-237	-252
		Amaretto	457	500	-163	-110
	Espresso	Caffe Mocha	1,419	1,512	-511	-528
		Decaf Espresso	950	945	-430	-365
	Herbal Tea	Chamomile	1,433	1,430	-137	-130
		Lemon	582	719	-198	-181
		Mint	399	430	-21	-40
	Tea	Darjeeling	1,050	1,155	20	35
		Earl Grey	991	1,075	81	55
		Green Tea	77	87	-13	-3

Product Type
- ■ Coffee
- ■ Espresso
- ■ Herbal Tea
- ■ Tea

2. **<u>*Highlight Table*</u>**- useful for emphasizing the range of values in a table by using color, while still allowing easy access to the detailed values. In the following table, notice how quickly you can see that 2007 was much less profitable relative to plan than 2008, Coffee was the worst relative performer in both years, and Tea was the best relative performer in both years.

A Highlight Table example showing *Profit as a % of Plan* by *Product Type* for *Year* and *Quarter*

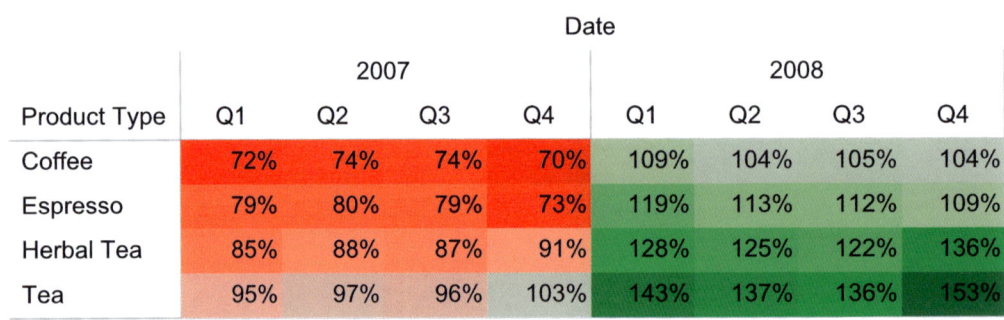

	Date							
	2007				2008			
Product Type	Q1	Q2	Q3	Q4	Q1	Q2	Q3	Q4
Coffee	72%	74%	74%	70%	109%	104%	105%	104%
Espresso	79%	80%	79%	73%	119%	113%	112%	109%
Herbal Tea	85%	88%	87%	91%	128%	125%	122%	136%
Tea	95%	97%	96%	103%	143%	137%	136%	153%

Profit as a % of Plan

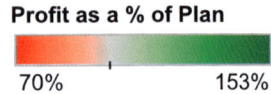

70%   153%

Heat Maps- how intense is it?

Heat Maps enable easy comparison of categorical values using color ranges. Use these when the specific values are less important than quickly identifying the trends based on the intensity or "temperature" of a measure, or when you have many members in several dimensions (e.g., all product sales and profits in all zip codes).

The layout is similar to a text table with variations in values encoded as colors. In the following heat map, you can quickly see a wide array of information. East is the biggest seller of Columbian (size of square). Caffe Mocha in the East was the only product to hit the profit plan target throughout 2007 (all green squares). Central is the biggest seller of Caffe Mocha (also size of square). West and South have significantly below profit plan products in 2008 (red squares).

A Heat Map showing *Profit as a Percent of Plan* (color-encoded) and *Sales* (size-encoded) by *Product* and *Market* for *Year* and *Quarter*

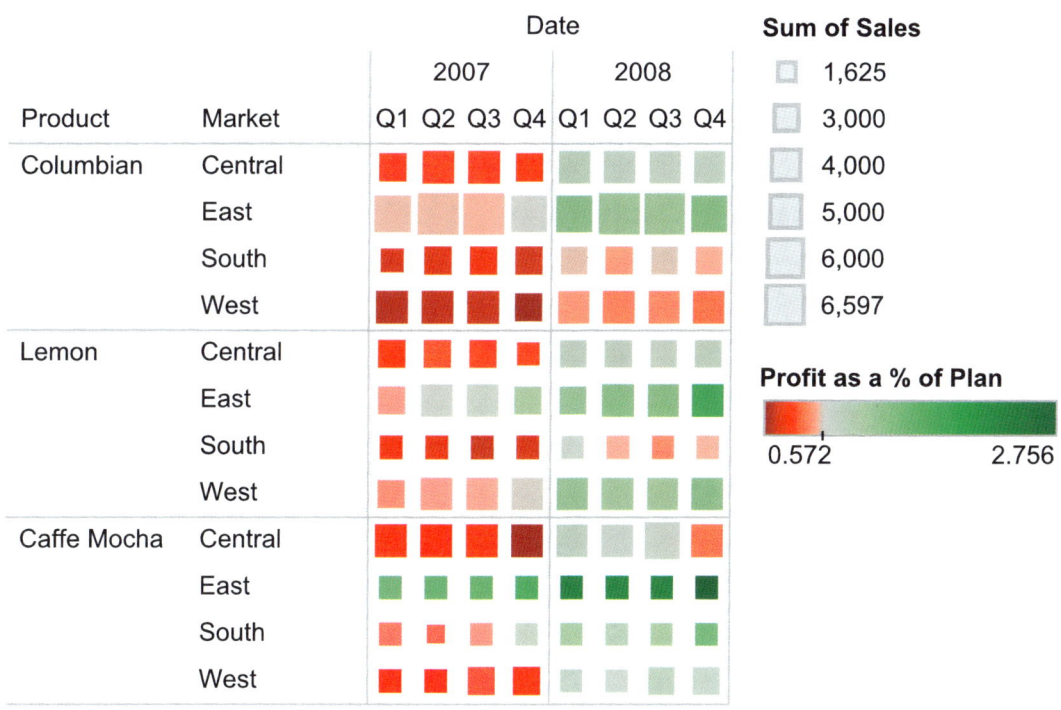

Bar Charts- five flavors to meet your needs

Bar Charts are the most flexible of the chart types and can be used for almost any visual analysis that involves categories or dimensions but does not require a text table- from dimensional comparisons to data ranking to data distribution to time series. As a bonus, bar charts are also very easy to digest since the human visual system is quite effective at understanding and rapidly comparing bar lengths.

Since bar charts encode the data values by the length of the bar, bar charts have one key constraint: Tableau must show the zero value on your measure axis or the analysis will be misleading. Fortunately, this occurs automatically in Tableau.

1. *Aligned Bar*- useful for comparing two or more measures across a dimension. The overall shape and trend of the bars can be compared, even when multiple measures are use on different scales or units of measure.

An Aligned Bar Chart for key US economic and tax measures by year, 1967-2007

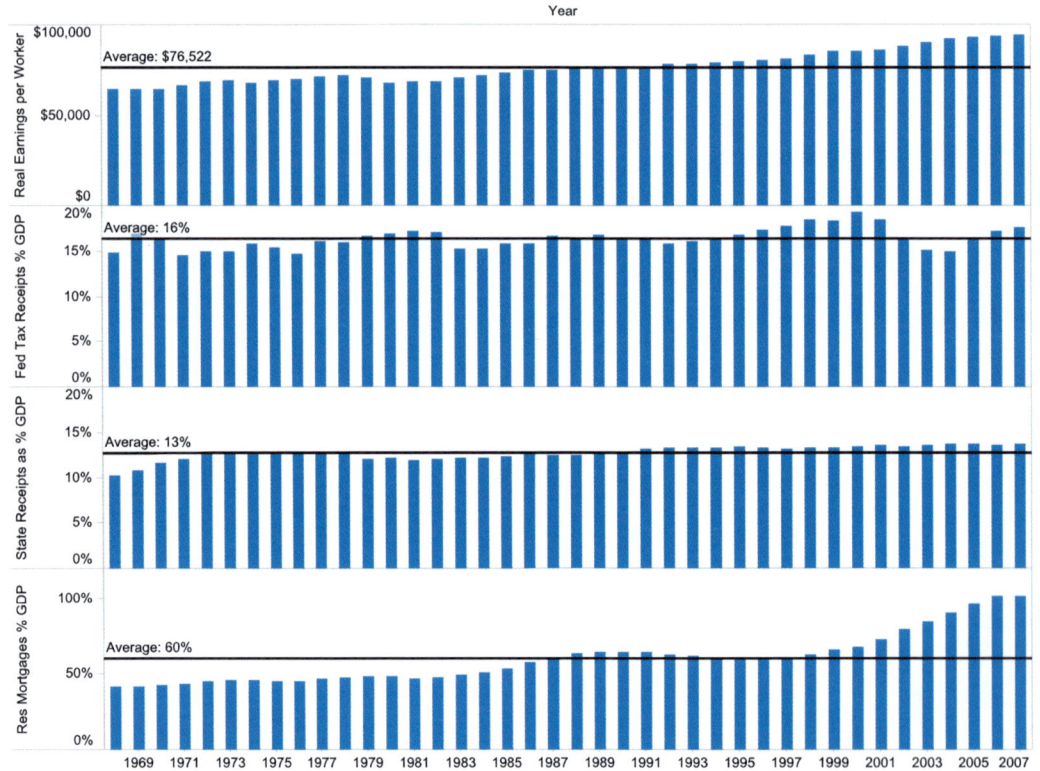

The sample aligned bar chart explores US economic data over 40 years, from 1968-2007. Beginning at the top of the view, the four measures shown are *Real Earnings per Worker* (adjusted to 2007 dollars), *Federal Tax Receipts as a Percent of GDP*, *State Tax Receipts as a Percent of GDP* and *Residential Mortgages (Outstanding) as a Percent of GDP*. A reference line has been added to each pane to represent the average of the pane across the 40- year period, allowing quick comparison within each pane relative to the overall measure average.

Key observations from this aligned bar view:

- The increase in *Real Earnings per Worker* is very impressive over the 50-year period.

- *Federal Tax Receipts as a Percent of GDP* has varied over the period, but not by more than a few percent less or more than the average.

- *State Tax Receipts as a Percent of GDP* also has varied, but appear to have increased more consistently than *Federal Tax Receipts as a Percent of GDP*.

- *Residential Mortgages as a Percent of GDP* has grown in spurts with radical growth in the last 8 years, driving them way above the historic average.

- *Federal versus State Tax Receipts as a Percent of GDP* are closer than popular perception, an average of 16% versus just 3% of GDP less for state receipts at 13%.

- The biggest concern after examining this view is the radical growth in *Residential Mortgages as a Percent of GDP*. Perhaps lower interest rates could temper this growth, but this definitely warrants further research.

2. ___Stacked Bar___- good for showing overall trend across categories or over time while simultaneously comparing the trend within categories for absolute measures. If you have an aligned bar chart with have many categories that requiring extensive scrolling to review, a stacked bar chart can be a good alternative.

A Stacked Bar Chart of *Profit* by *Quarter* and *Region* within each *Quarter*

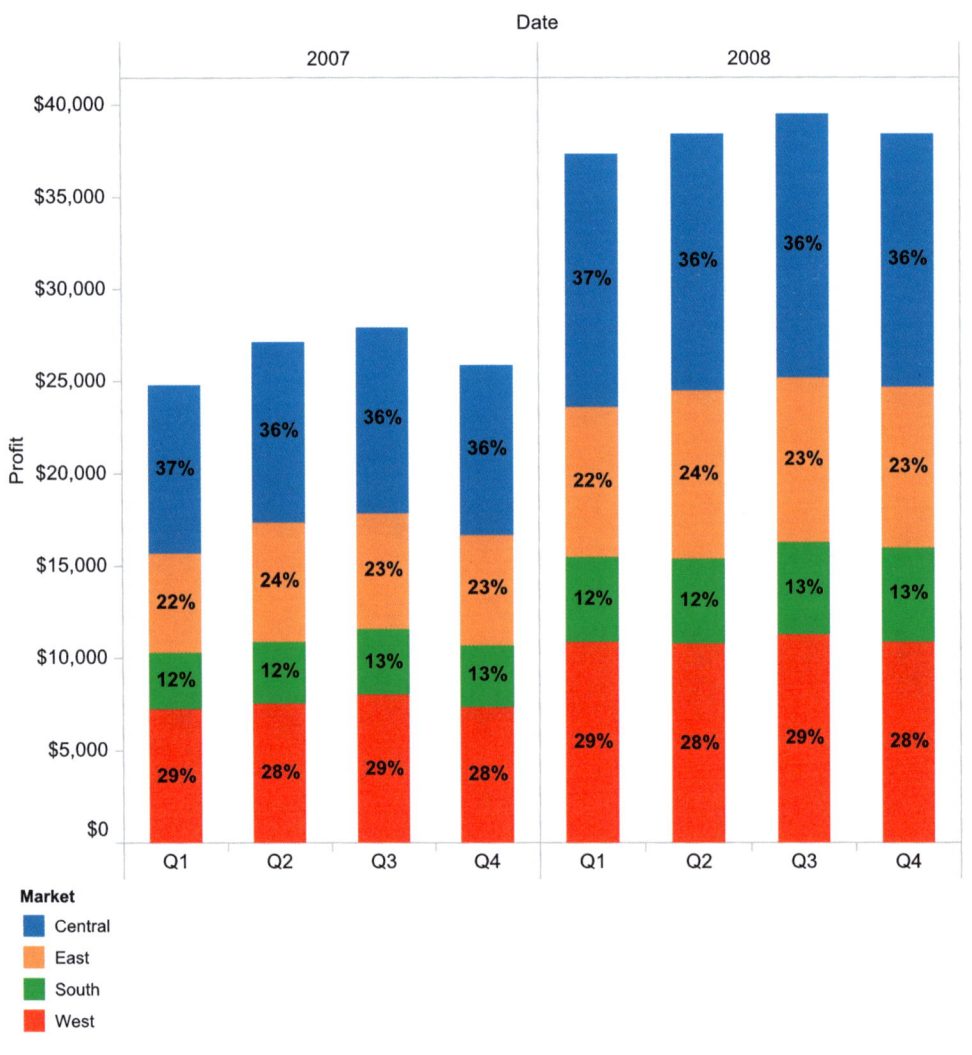

3. <u>**Side-by-Side Bar**</u>- while aligned bars are generally superior, side-by-side bar charts can be useful when comparing similar measures within each cell.

A Side-by-Side Bar Chart of *Profit* and *Profit versus Plan* by *Year* and *Product Type*

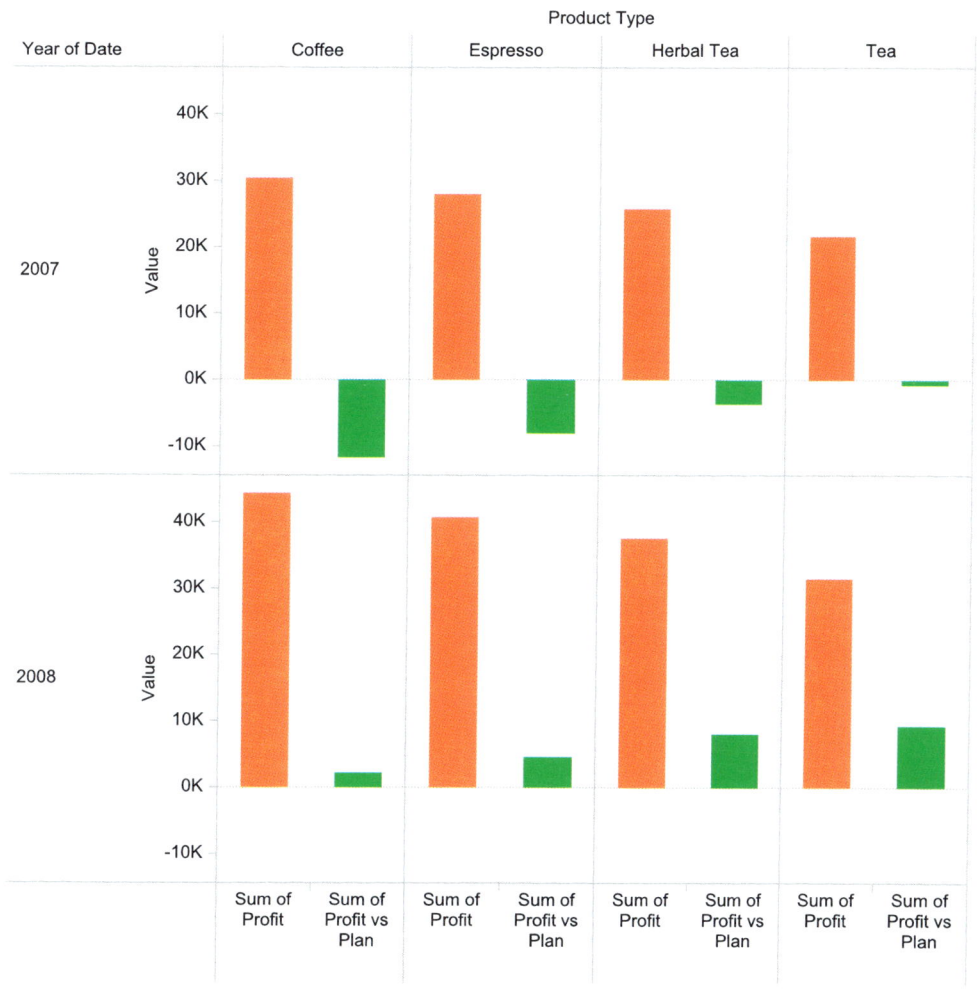

4. ___Bar with Measure on Color___- another alternative to the aligned bar chart. In addition to the related primary measure (bar length), color encoding can be useful for understanding intensity of a measure, as shown in the following view.

A Bar Chart With Measure on Color of *Profit* and *Profit versus Plan* by *Year* and *Product Type*

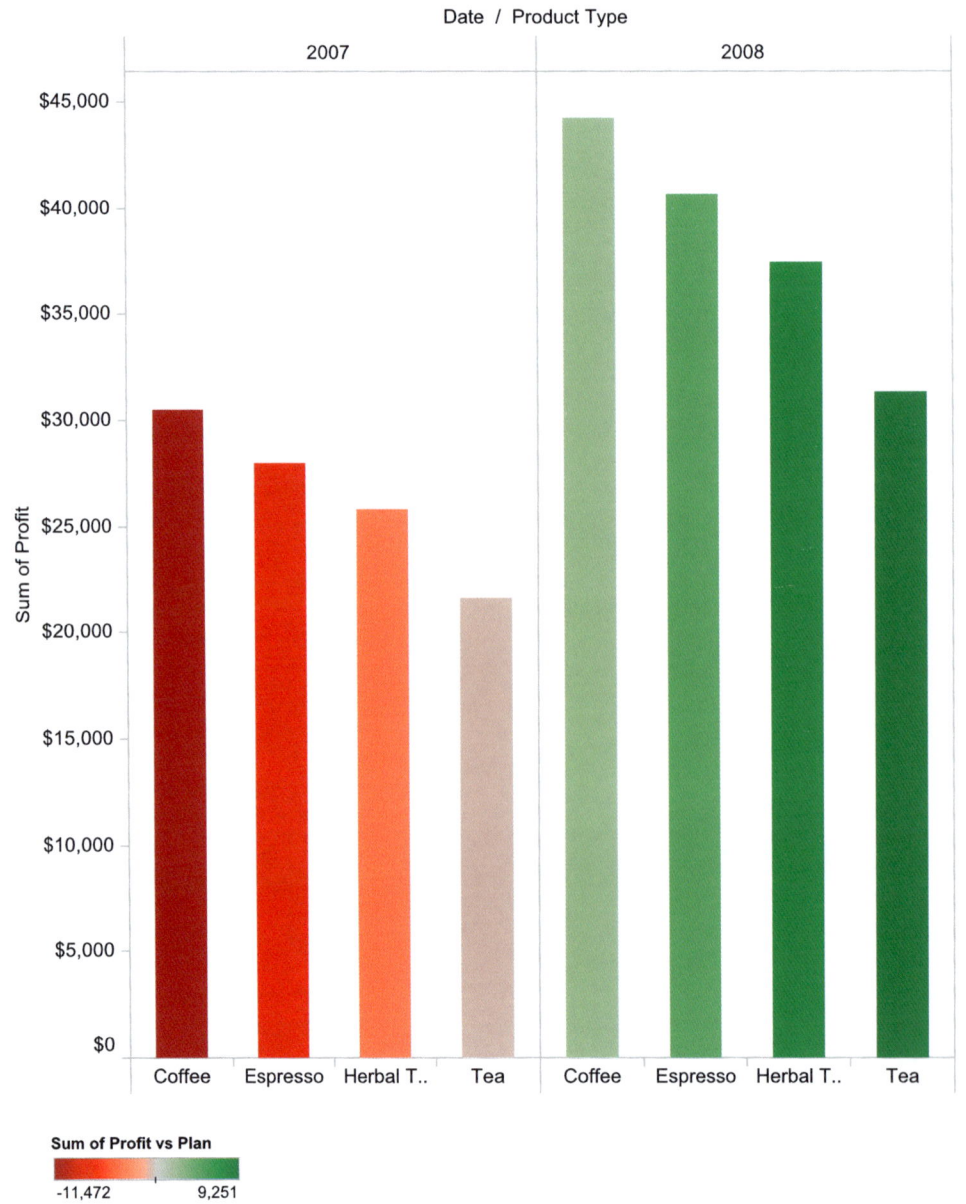

5. **<u>Histogram</u>**- a specialized bar chart that displays frequencies of a value or range of values. By convention, these are usually vertical (up and down) bars. A histogram is useful for examining the distribution of occurrences.

A Histogram showing number of occurrences of annual unemployment rates, 1968-2007

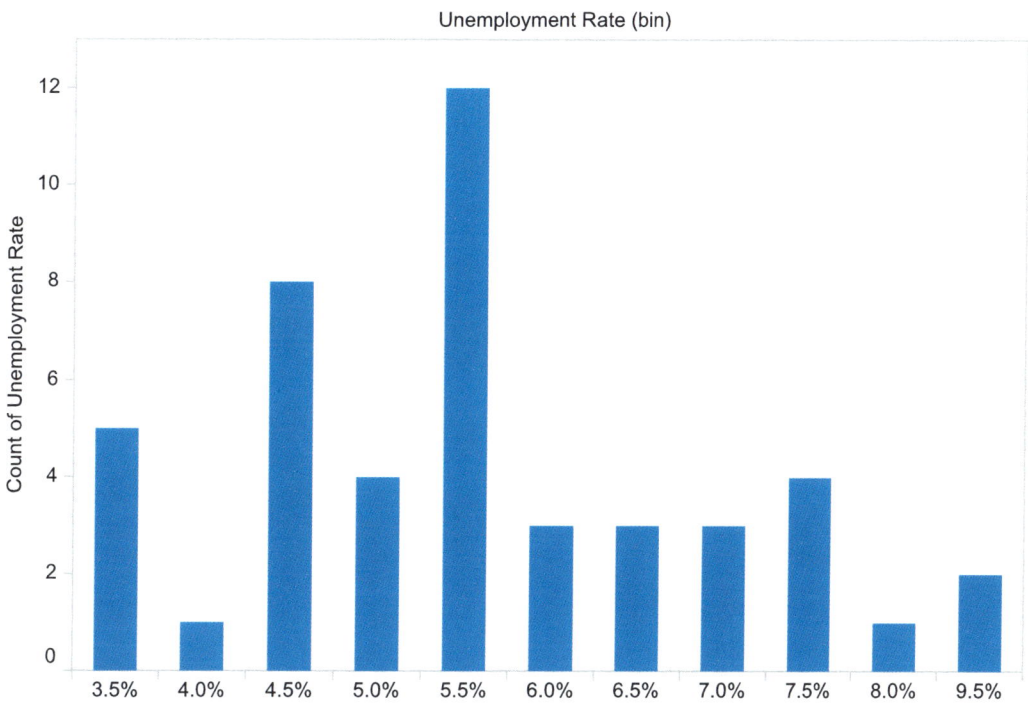

An enhanced histogram with Trend Line- annual unemployment rates by presidential party, 1968-2007

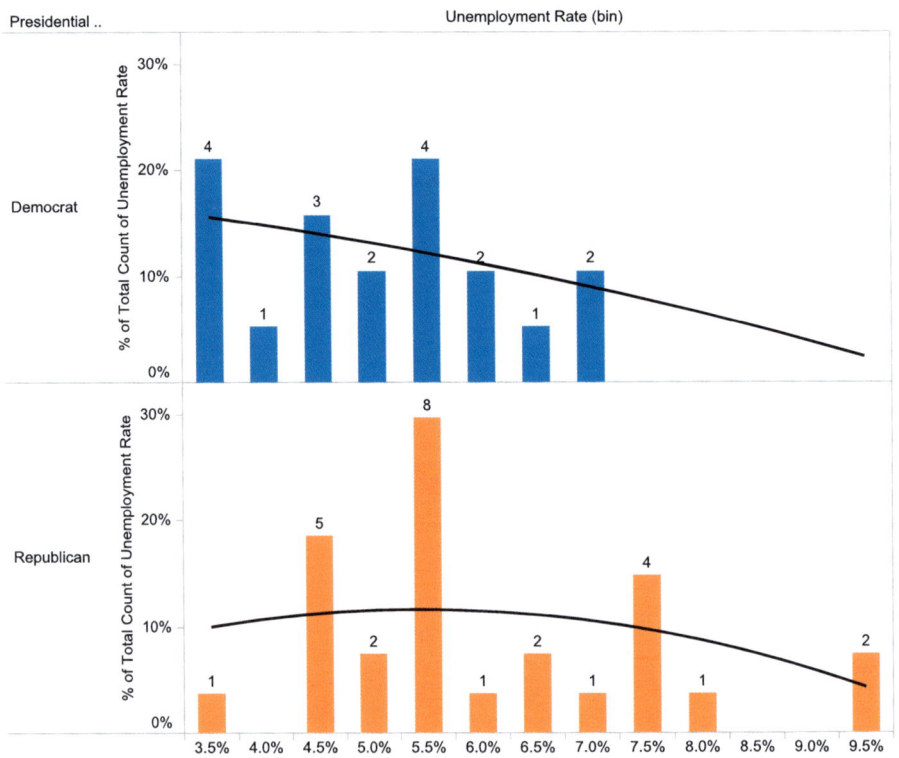

Chapter 5

Creating and managing advanced Views

Chapter Highlights

- Understanding the five advanced view categories in Tableau

    o Line Charts- once upon a time

    o Scatter Plots- do they move together?

    o Gantt Chart- time after time

    o Pie Chart- a surprise that may please some

    o Maps (Geographic)- where did that happen?

Views are the foundation of Tableau, so mastering them is the key to optimizing your visualization insights. In Chapter 4, you learned about the basic view types. This chapter explains the advanced view types.

In Tableau, you can use the "Show Me!" button to display the array of seventeen specific view types. Tableau automatically highlights the view that it "guesses" will be most useful for the data items that you selected, and lets you know which other views are available. Views that are not appropriate due to the nature of your selected data items are grayed out on the Show Me! dialog.

If you accept the "Show Me!" view, you can easily change the view type later via "Show Me" or by your own manual modifications to the shelves and settings. In fact, when you manually adjust your view, Tableau may surprise you by automatically changing it to the appropriate one - that is the beauty of Tableau!

I have grouped the seventeen templates into eight logical categories for your convenience. In this chapter, the five advanced view categories are covered. Please note the view templates are addressed in the same order as depicted in the Show Me! dialog box. The following table summarizes nine of the seventeen view types and the data items required to use them as the basis of a view.

View Category / Name	View Example	Required Dimension Items	Required Measure Items
Line Chart- Line (Discrete)		1 date	1 or more
Line Chart- Line (Continuous)		1 date or continuous dimension	1 or more
Scatter Plot- Circle		1 or more	1 or more
Scatter Plot- Scatter (Single)		0 or more	2 to 4
Scatter Plot- Scatter (Matrix)		1 or more categorical	3 to 6
Scatter Plot- Dual Axis		1 or more	2 or more
Gantt Chart- Gantt		1 plus 1 continuous dimension or date	0
Pie Chart- Pie		1 or more	1 or more
Map- Map		1 geographic dimension plus 0 or more	1 or more

Line Charts- describe what happened recently

When a dimension field includes a date, "Show Me!" recommends a line chart because it is more effective than a bar chart for showing trends across multiple categories. The default is to treat the date dimension as a discrete variable, meaning that the next highest level of date data is used to break the lines into regions in the chart (see the 1st example below). Note that if you have several years of data, the default view is by year, if you drill down to quarter, the view is broken into regions by year.

1. **Line (Discrete)** - useful for showing trends over time across one or more categories. Notice in the example that 2007 and 2008 have different patterns for Regular coffee profits in addition to being higher overall year over year. By making the chart discrete in the view, it is easy to compare quarters across the year- Q3 in 2008 is very different for Regular coffee but similar for Decaf.

A Discrete Line Chart of Coffee Type Profits by Month, 2007-2008

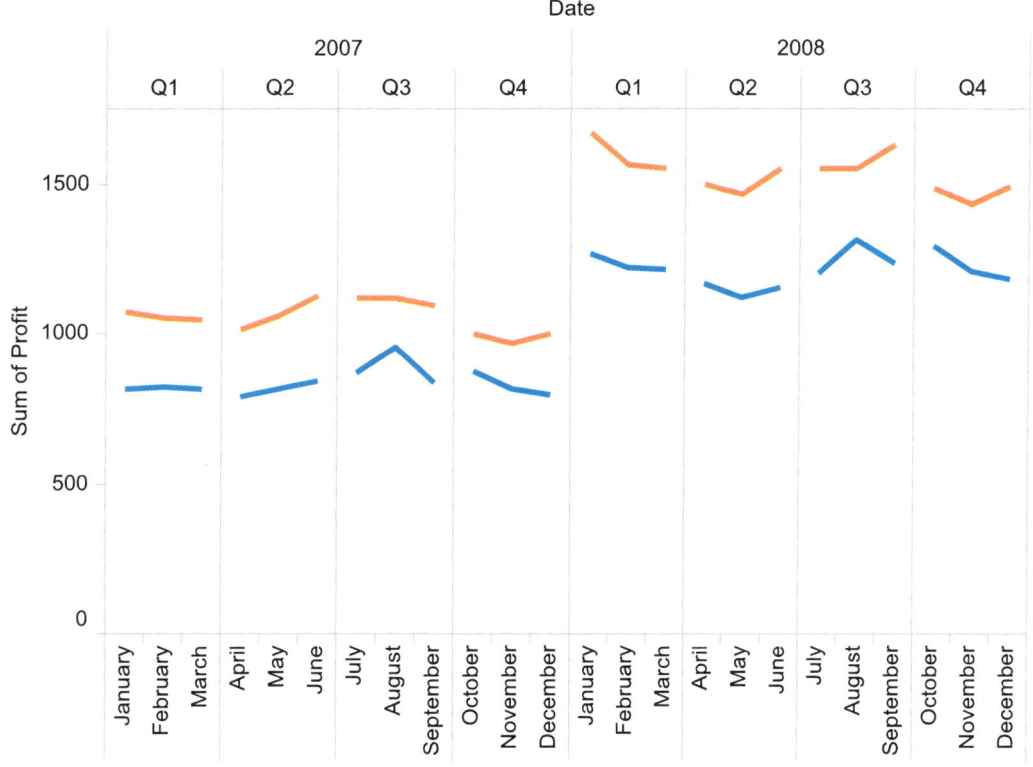

2. <u>***Line (Continuous)***</u> - Continuous line charts are useful at exploring the relationship of two continuous measures as shown below. While date data can be used, it is recommended to use a discrete line chart instead.

The example below clearly shows a very different product margin pattern for items shipped via delivery truck than via the other two modes, especially at the higher margin levels. Note that regular air shipments have a very pronounced peak at lower margin levels while the other two modes have less pronounced peaks in this range of margin.

A Continuous Line Chart showing *Sales* by *Product Margin Percent* categorized by *Mode of Shipment*

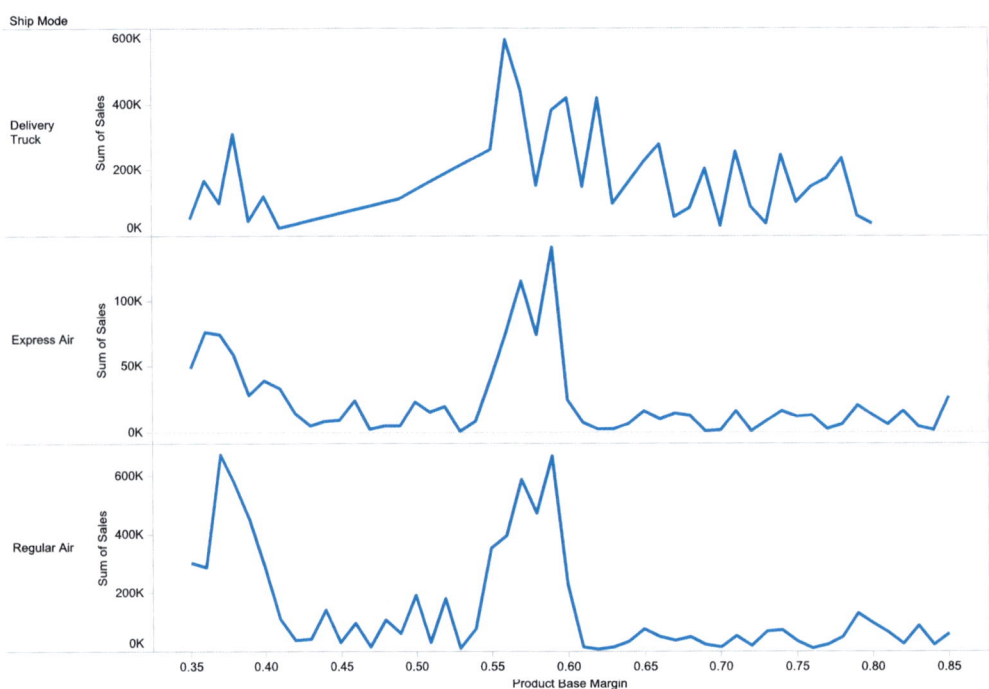

Scatter Plots- relationships matter

Scatter plots are very useful for understanding the relationship of one or more measures, often referred to as correlation. Scatter plots are very effective for comparing one or more measures and how the other measures vary across each measure and/or category. Tableau offers four distinct types of scatter plots.

1. *Circle*- the simplest form of scatter plot, highlighted by Show Me! when you select one or more dimensional items that are not date or location related and one measure. The example shown here does an excellent job of highlighting the similarity of average profit in the Furniture category in all the regions except the East. Additionally, the wide range of average profitability for technology products encourages further investigation to uncover ideas for improvement in some of the regions.

A Circle Scatter Plot of *Average Profit* by *Region* and *Product Category*

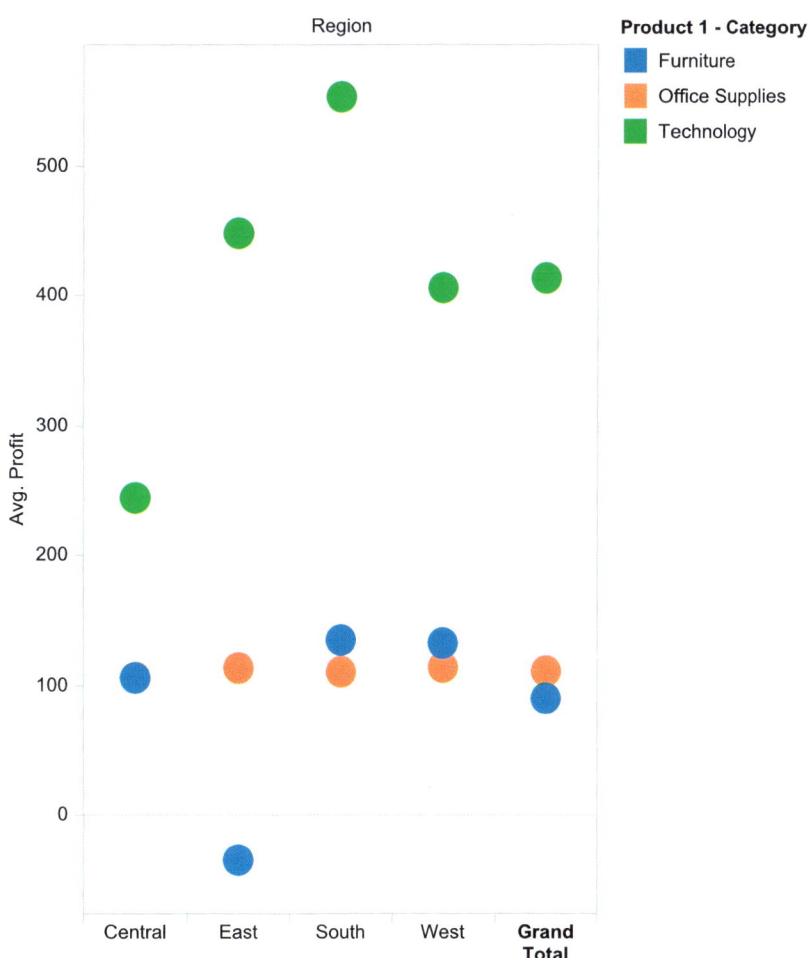

2. ***Scatter (Single)*** - compares two or more measures and at least one dimension. The example contains a rich amount of information. The biggest selling product/order priority combinations are not always the most profitable combinations. Urgent shipments often take more time to ship than lower priority shipments (not good). Only the Central region has the most profitable shipments in the low priority group. The Central region makes the highest profit orders wait the longest (both by profit and order priority!).

A Single Scatter Plot of *Average Profit* by *Sales* across *Region- Average Time to Ship* Size-encoded and *Order Priority* Color-encoded

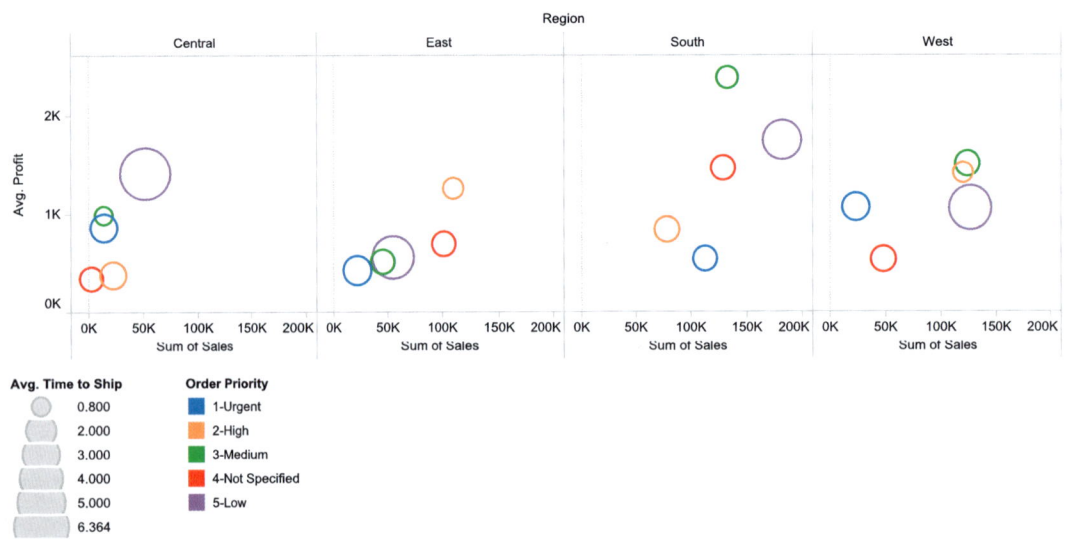

3. **_Scatter (Matrix)_** - useful for comparing several measures against one another. All measures are placed on a "grid" (matrix) of multiple scatter plots- every measure is shown against every other measure (including itself) to allow simultaneous viewing of multiple relationships. Each measure can be examined across either the horizontal axis (also known as the X-axis) or the vertical axis (also known as the Y-axis) against every other measure. In Tableau 5, selecting a point highlights it in all the other scatter plots, which makes it simple to see how an outlier in one plot performs in the other plots. Therefore, you can look at the inverted data, which is useful for examining the relationships from two perspectives visually. Additionally, one or more dimensions may be encoded in the plots using color or shape to understand the impact of categorical data across the plots.

   The example that follows compares various consumer price indices (CPI) by year. The years are also color-encoded by decade.

A Matrix Scatter Plot of three components of the Consumer Price Index-decade of occurrence is Color-encoded

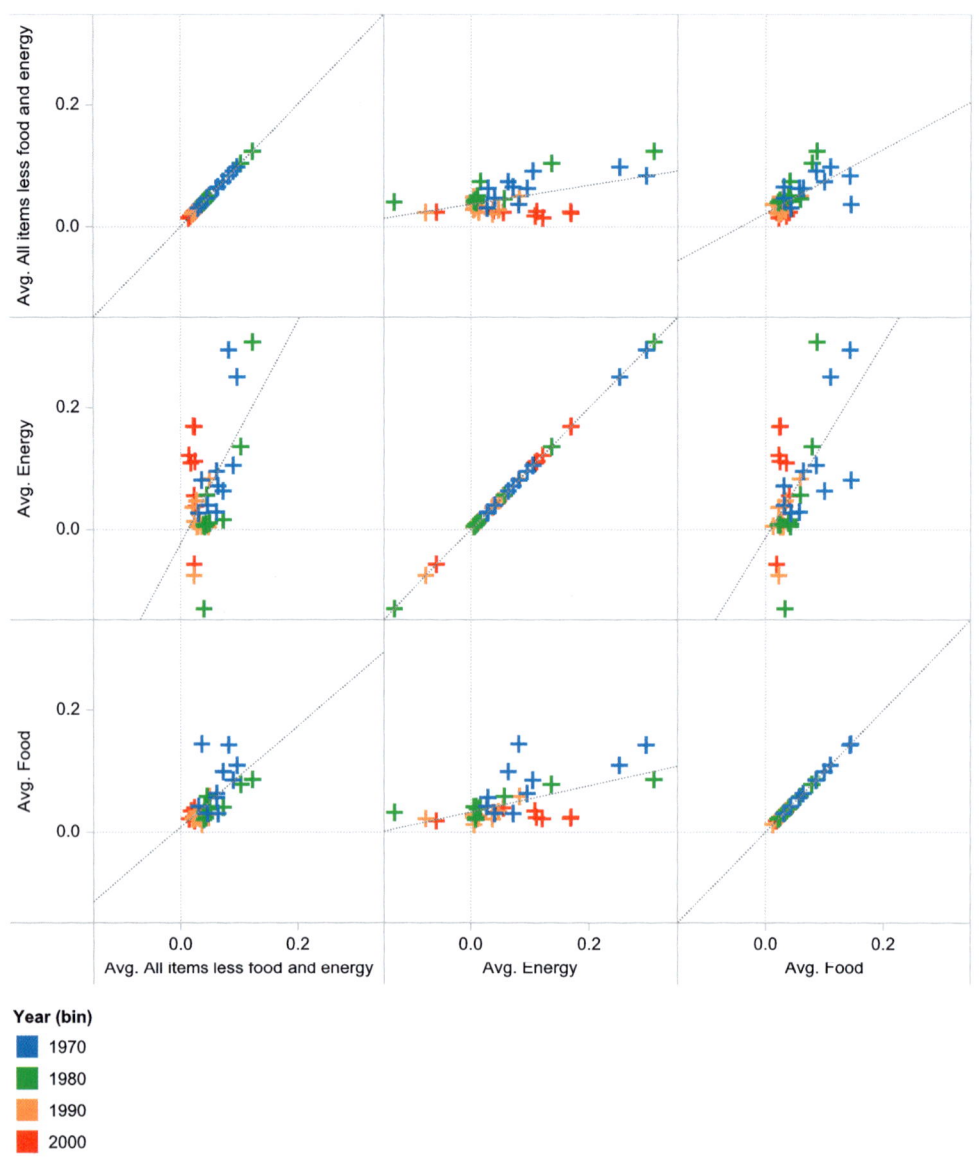

Year (bin)
- 1970
- 1980
- 1990
- 2000

The three measures are *All items less food and energy* (located at the top on the vertical axis and the left on horizontal axis), *Energy* (the middle on both axes) and *Food* (the bottom on the vertical axis and the right on the horizontal axis).

Starting in the bottom middle plot, you can see that in years when the *Energy* CPI is higher, the *Food* CPI is also higher. The trend line shows an approximate relationship, with the growth rate of food prices being higher in high-energy price years, but the rate of growth is slower than energy prices, by about half.

Moving just one plot to the left, you can see that as **_All items less food and energy_** move up, that **_Food_** prices move up almost in unison. There are two years that are outliers, 1973 and 1974 (if this graph was in Tableau right now, you could see the specific year by hovering the cursor over the data points in the view.) Examining the same information inverted in the upper right plot shows that there might be a more complex shape to this relationship, which may be worth further investigation and analysis.

Finally, moving to the second row and first column, you can see that **_All items less food and energy_** have a nearly vertical relationship with energy price changes. There does appear to be a number of years with some linear pattern but also a number of outlier years in multiple decades. This warrants further research before reaching conclusions about whether or not a relationship exists.

4. **_Dual Axis_**- useful for examining two or more relevant measures that have different units of measurement (e.g., dollars sold and units sold.) Via shape- and/or color-encoding, the different measurements can be displayed in the same scatter plot, enabling easy comparison of multiple measures.

The example showing a dual axis scatter plot displays individual customers frequently receiving higher than average discounts. For each customer, *Average Discount* is color-encoded as blue and scaled to the left axis, while *Total Profit* is orange and scaled to the right axis.

A Dual Axis Scatter Plot of High Discount customers- *Average Discount* and *Total Profit*, With *Total Sales* Size-Encoded

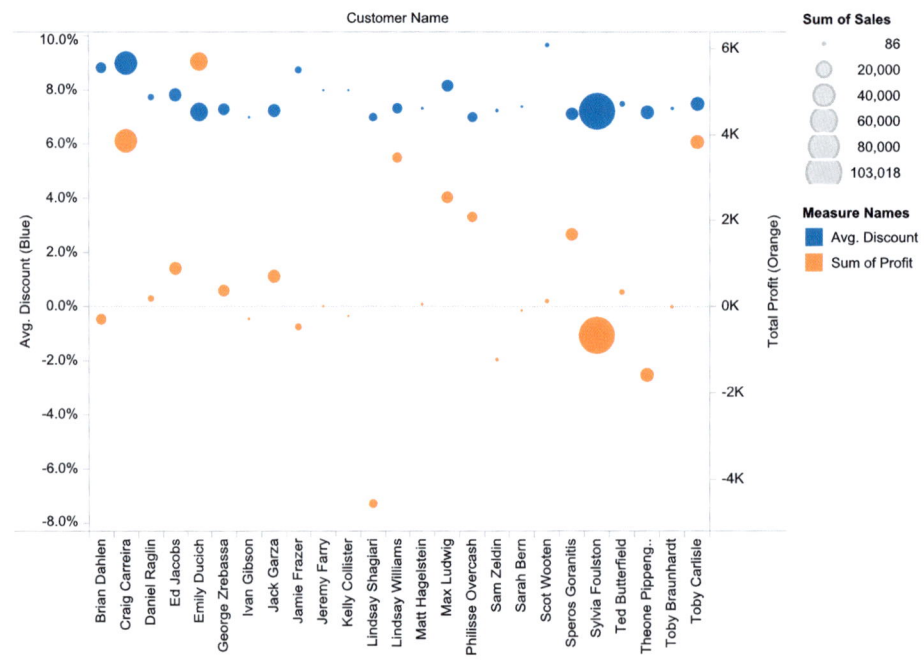

The bubble size encodes the total sales to each customer, ranging from $86 to $103,018! Examining the dual axis scatter plot, you can see that a significant number of these high discount customers are unprofitable- with the biggest profit loser one of the lower sales amount customers (Sylvia Foulston)!

Adding a Row Grand Total to this plot (not pictured here) shows that in total these customers are profitable- $16,399 of profit on $311,160 of sales. The **Select toolbar** or **Filter function** (covered later in this book), was used to create the next figure showing a subset of the view with only the negative profit customers.

Filtered View of High Discount customers- displaying negative profitability customers only, Row Grand Totals added

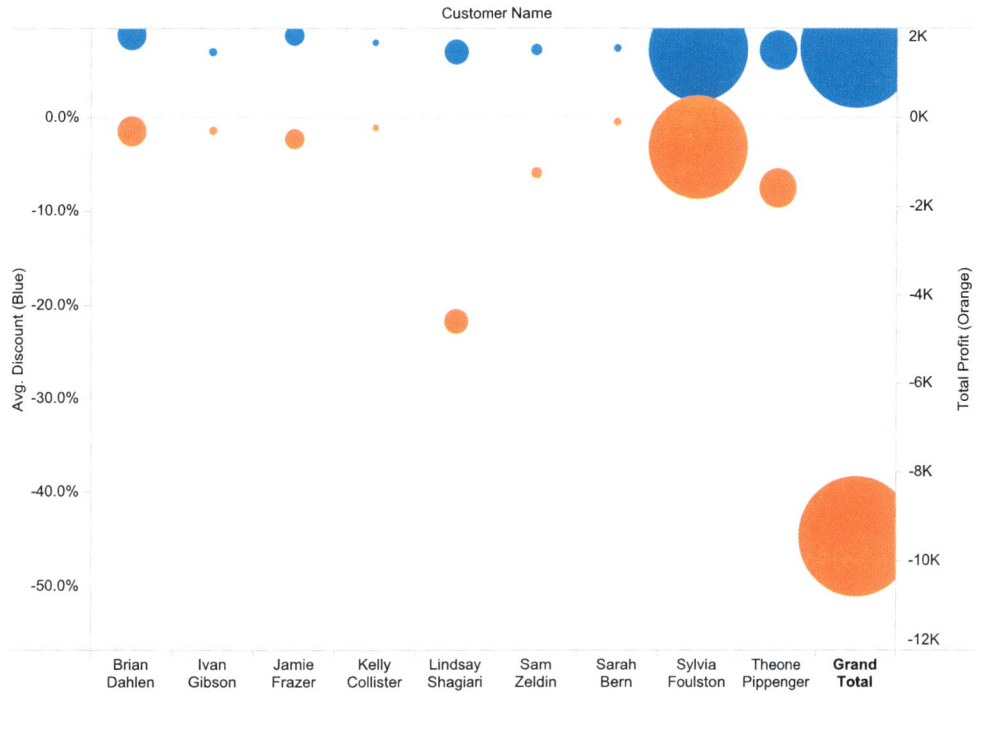

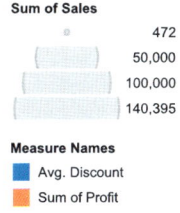

It is possible to see that negative profit customers result in a loss of $9,429 on sales of $140,395. If we can more effectively manage these high discount/profit loss customers, it may be possible to improve profitability among the high discount group while simultaneously reducing unprofitable sales transactions. Further investigation is necessary to identify an ideal course of action.

Gantt Chart- understand the details over time

Gantt charts are a specialized type of chart that can be very useful at showing repeated events over time or a range of another continuous dimension. Creating these for the first time can be confusing if you use the Show Me! button. Show Me! restricts the Column axis (horizontal or X-axis) to continuous dimension items and the Row axis (vertical or Y-axis) to discrete dimension items- neither can be a measure item!

The example that follows is a slightly modified Gantt chart (in a classic Gantt chart, the bars would be varying widths to represent a second time dimension, such as "time to delivery" placed on the size shelf). This chart displays *Time to Ship* for various orders in a company. The *Ship Date* of each shipment is shown in the chart and the *Ship mode* is color-encoded. The rows of the chart along the Y-axis show the number of days required for the shipment to arrive at the customer **relative to the date the order was received.**

A Gantt Chart of time to ship in the South region, August 2007 – August 2008

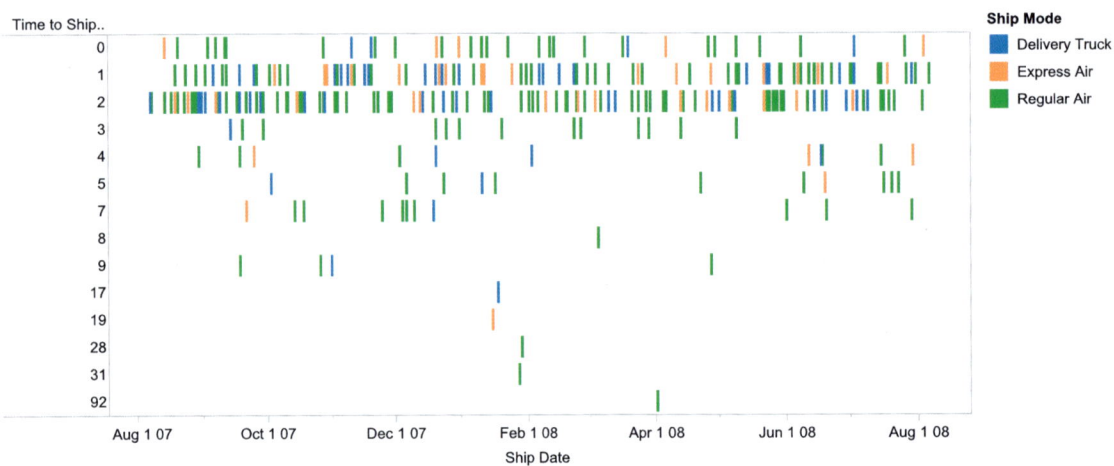

Examining this chart yields great insight into troubled shipments, taking up to 92 days to arrive. By backtracking from the arrival dates, you can determine that most of these were sent out in the early part of 2008. The three slowest shipments were all sent via Regular Air. Examining the arrival dates, they all appear to have been ordered in early January. Therefore, it appears that orders placed in early January is a good place to start examining the extreme outliers with respect to company delivery time.

Pie Charts- by popular demand

Tableau having a Pie Chart view is akin to chickens having a pet hawk- very unexpected! Tableau likely added this view type due to popular customer demand, in spite of the well-known minimal utility of this view type. Both Edward Tufte and Stephen Few (highly respected experts in data visualization) rail against the overuse of this chart type and with good cause- they are frequently misleading and inappropriate for effectively conveying information. Unfortunately, they are popular in business applications due to earlier graphics programs that emphasized this chart type due to their "appetite" appeal- after all, who doesn't like pie? The easiest fallback from a pie chart habit is a bar chart, which are typically superior at conveying the information in your data.

A good rule to remember when using pie charts is to limit the number of slices shown to five or less. If you have more than five slices, you should use the grouping capability of Tableau to reduce the less important slices past the top four into one "Other" slice. Another serious issue with pie charts is the fact that measures with negative values, averages, minimums, maximums, etc. will be very misleading in the slices- so avoid them at all costs if you have measures with negative values (like profitability, shown below to illustrate the issue at the pie size level.)

Given the limitations, the example below shows a relatively useful application of pie charts, but one that is rarely used. The example shows *Profit* of an office equipment firm across *Region*, *Product Category*, and *Customer Segment*- with the overall size of the pie conveying the overall profit level at the intersection of *Region* and *Product Category*.

A grid of Pie Charts showing *Profit* (overall pie size) by *Region, Product,* and *Customer Segment*

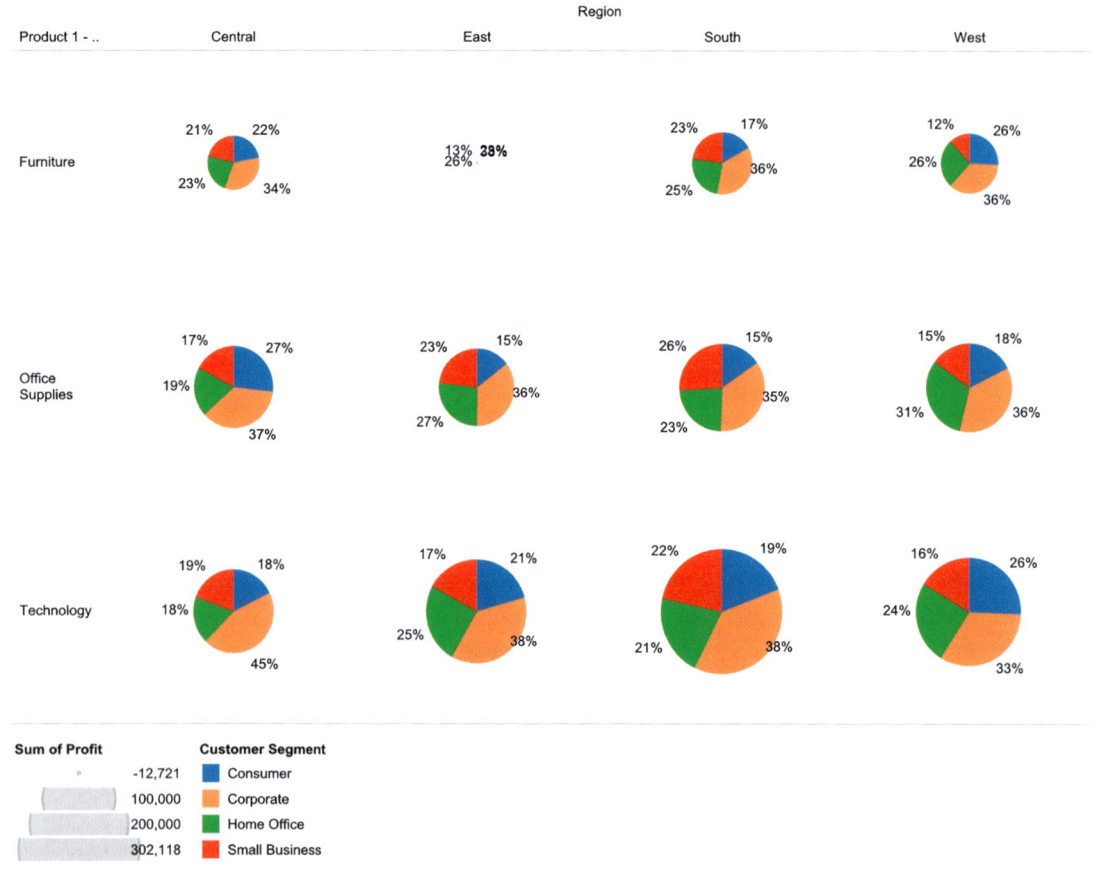

 It is relatively easy to see that the South region has the most profitable product line with technology products, since it is the largest pie, and that corporate customers are the most profitable in every region/product intersection, as the orange corporate "slices" are always the largest.

One oddity is the fact that the East/furniture intersection is actually negative profitability! How can a pie be a negative size since the area of the pie is supposed to convey the significance of the pie? Tableau attempts to overcome this deficiency of pie charts by making the pie nearly invisible, which is a good compromise if you must use pie charts, but the best solution would be to use a different view type.

Geographic Maps- where did it happen?

Maps with size- or color-encoded shapes are available if your dataset has country, state, or postal code level data available. These are particularly useful if you want to convey the spatial distribution of one or more measures. You can also display the measures over various dimension categories across multiple views of the map.

The sample map shows social insurance data from 2006 for the United States divided by state. The two metrics displayed are *percent of social insurance paid <u>to</u> the residents of a state* over *percent of social insurance paid <u>by</u> the residents of a state* (size-encoded) and the *social insurance dollar amount paid out per person in the state* (color-encoded).

Federal government social insurance payout (2006) as a *Percent of Social Insurance Paid* (Square Size) and *Total Dollars Spent per Person* (Color-Encoded)

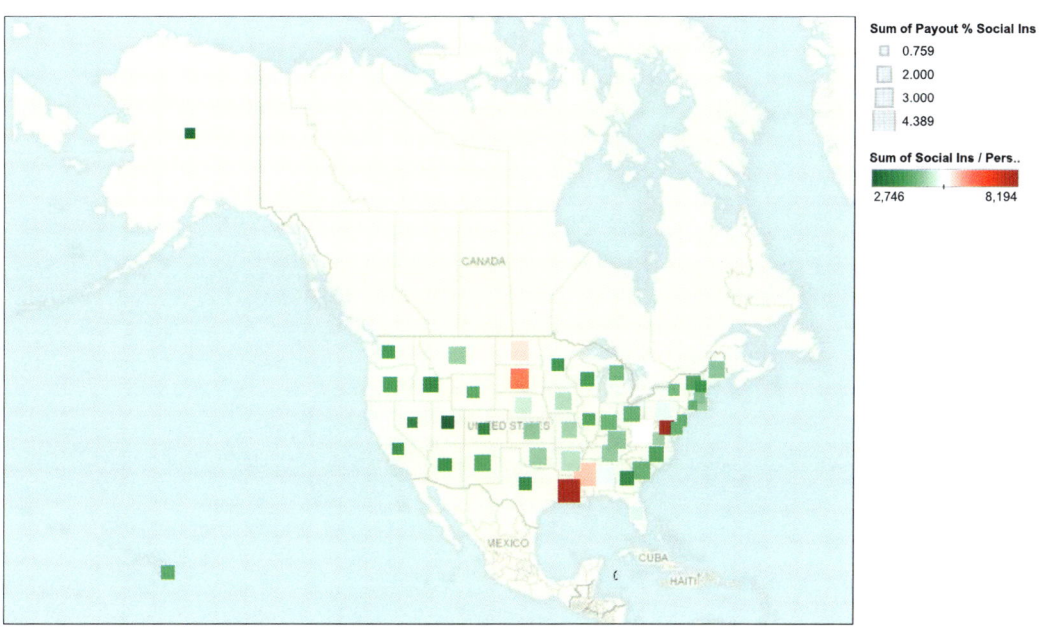

Examining this map yields some interesting regional information- the red squares identify which states have a high proportion of net inflows from federal social insurance programs. Louisiana is the highest on the payout scale relative to dollars paid into social insurance programs, probably due to Hurricane Katrina in 2005. Additionally, Mississippi and the Dakotas have high payout ratios. Looking at the square size, you can see that these same states also have large absolute dollar inflows per person, but so does the District of Columbia, one addition to the former list. Effectively, this map shows net subsidies from wealthier states to generally less wealthy states.

Page intentionally left blank for proper book pagination.

Chapter 6

Taking over with Tableau - View structure, visual appearance, Summaries, Formatting and Titles

---

Chapter Highlights

- Customizing Views Using the Columns, Rows, Pages and Filters Shelves

- Enhance Your Visual Appeal with the Marks Card

- The Summary Card- Rapid Data Insights

- Headers and Axes

- Titles, Captions, Field Labels, Legends

- Formatting Values in Your Views

This chapter reviews many of the capabilities of Tableau that take you beyond the powerful Show Me! defaults and empower you to customize and even build your own views from scratch.

In this chapter, you will be prompted several times to return to the default view. To create this view, **open the Sample Coffee Chain dataset and select the following three data items by keeping the <Ctrl> key depressed:** *Market*, *Product Type* **and** *Profit*. **Click Show Me!** and keep the default selection, Aligned Bar Chart, **click OK**.

Default view: Aligned Bar Chart

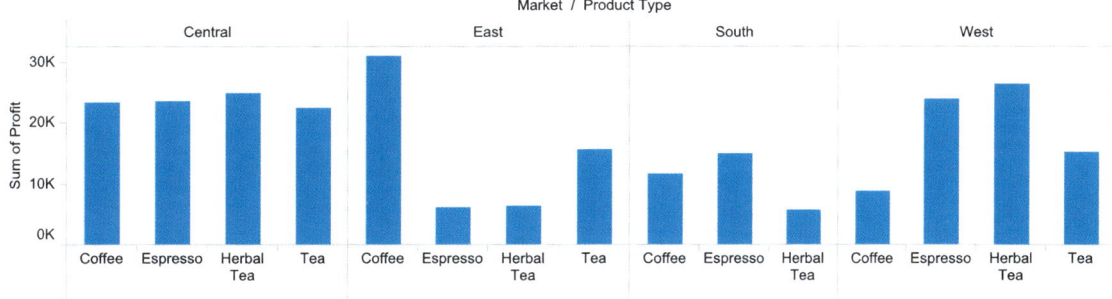

Customizing Views from Columns, Rows, Pages and Filters Shelves

In this section, you will learn to manually create or modify views via the Columns, Rows, Pages, and Filters shelves, which are located underneath the toolbar to the right of the Data Items pane.

1. <u>*Columns*</u>: when you place data items on the Columns shelf, you create the vertical column aspect of the view. Depending on which data items you choose, you can subdivide the view into vertical columns by determining which values are included on the X-axis (horizontal axis). **Drag and drop *Date* to the right of *Product Type* in the Columns shelf.** The chart type automatically changes from Aligned Bar to Line (Discrete).

   !*Alternate Route*: Move the *date* field to the first position on the Columns shelf to see a different view of the data. Tableau is all about discovery, so feel free to experiment and move data items around in the examples to see how the insights change!

Modifying the view by placing *Date* on the Columns shelf

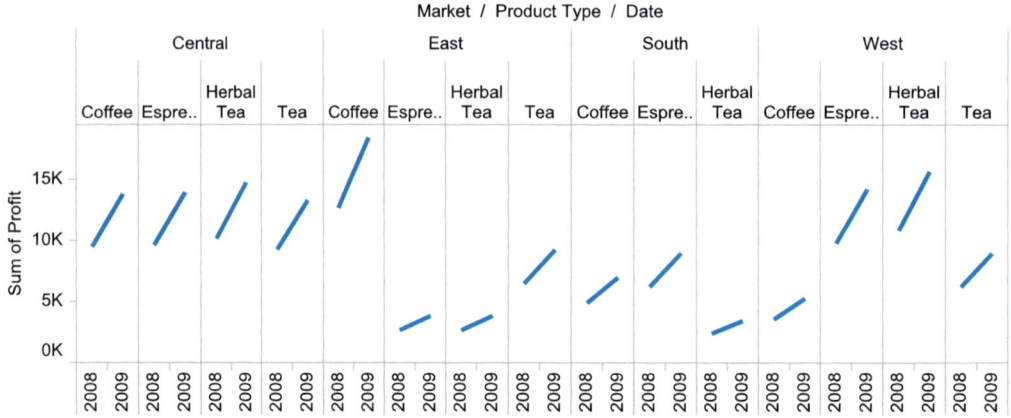

2. **Rows**: determines the values shown horizontally across the rows of the view. Using the Rows shelf, you can partition your chart into horizontal groups by choosing what is included on the Y-axis (vertical axis). **Add *Market Size* to the left of *SUM(Profit)* on the Rows shelf.**

Modifying the view by placing *Market Size* on the Rows shelf

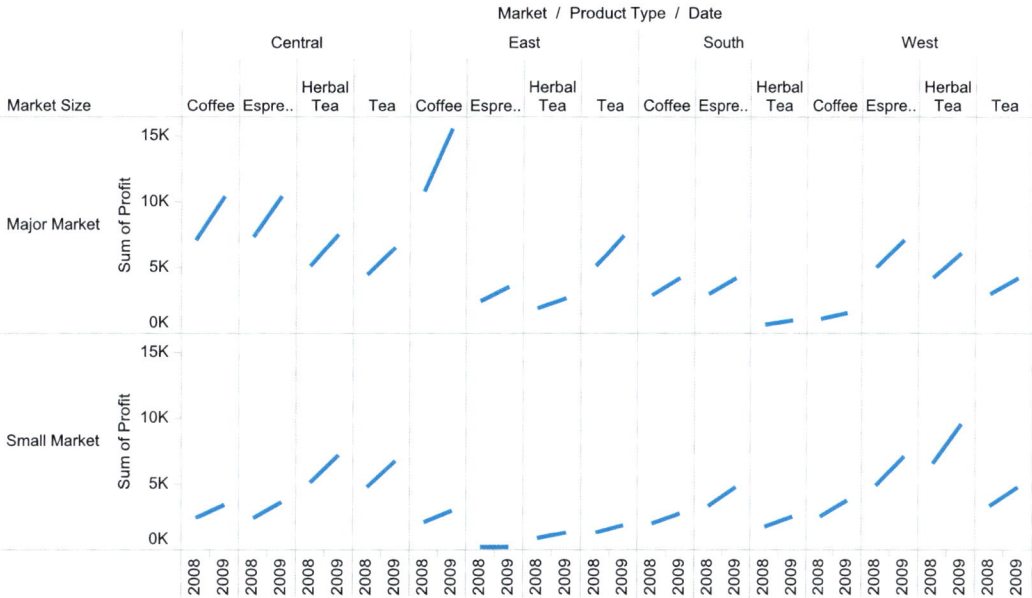

3. <u>**Pages**</u>: if you add a data item to the Pages shelf, you subset the complete view that displays all of the values of that data item into multiple views available on different "pages". The Pages feature allows you to scroll through the various page item values or across time. When you export, print, or publish the view, it will only display the currently selected page (similar to a filter, except that the number of rows and columns does not change across pages).

Add *Type* to the Pages shelf. Underneath the Pages shelf, the Current Page Card appears, with Decaf displayed in both the drop-down menu and the view. If you click the down carat next to Decaf, you can see that the other available *Type* is Regular. You can change to the Regular view in four ways: **by choosing Regular from the drop-down menu, clicking on the arrow directly to the right, moving the arrow on the progress bar in the middle of the card to the right, or using the scroll bar found on the bottom left of the card.** The three buttons found on the bottom right of the card are used to adjust the speed at which the view changes between Decaf and Regular, in case you would like to make visual comparisons between the two.

Data item *Type* on the Pages shelf, page controls below data item

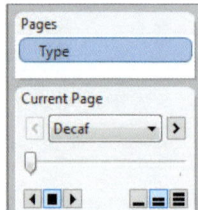

Modifying the view by placing *Type* on the Pages shelf- Decaf shown

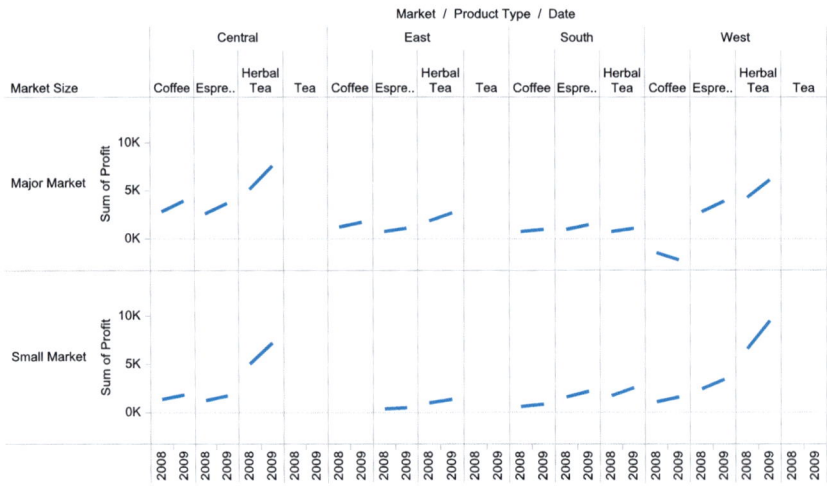

4. *Filters*: using the filters shelf can help you focus on what you need and accelerate query time by reducing both the data retrieved from the data source and the data displayed in the view. For instance, you may only want to look at particular dates, products, or locations and exclude others from the current view. **Add *Product* to the Filters shelf. A dialog box will pop up- from the General tab, click on the Values dropdown and change the setting to "Use All" (you could manually specify which products to further filter here, but we want the top 3 overall), then click on the tab labeled Top, select By Field -> Top -> 3 -> Profit -> Sum -> OK.**

Modifying the view by placing *Product* on the Filters shelf

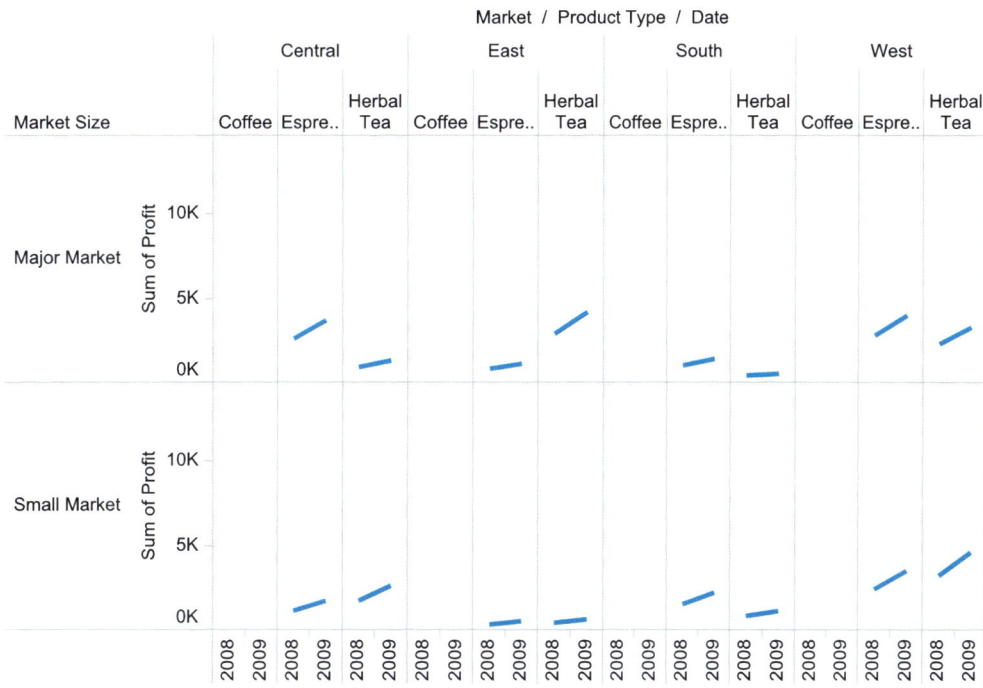

Enhance visual appeal with the Marks card

As shown in previous chapters, the Marks card has a variety of functions that help you build exactly the right view. A mark represents a row (or group of rows) of data from your original dataset. With the Marks card, you can design the look of these marks by placing data items on the Text, Color, Size, Shape and Level of Detail shelves.

Please reset your view to the default layout shown at the beginning of this chapter by selecting *Market*, *Product Type* and *Profit*, clicking Show Me!, and then clicking OK. Then place *Market* on the Filters shelf. When the dialog box pops up, uncheck South and click OK. This removes South from the view and retains Central, East and West.

! *Alternate Route*: Right-click on South and select Exclude. Alternatively, click on *Market* on the Filter shelf, select Show Quick Filter and check South on the *Market* filter card that appears on the right side of the view.

1. **_Text_**: this allows you to select which type of aggregate value, such as sum, average, count, etc., that you would like to represent a specific variable or metric to either display in cross tabs or summarize data items in charts. The basic use of the text feature is to highlight the same variable or metric with different aggregate values.

Add *Profit* to the Text shelf. Click on the down carat in the Text shelf, scroll down to Measure (Sum) and change the aggregate function from Sum to Average.

Modifying the view by placing *Profit* on the Text shelf and changing the aggregate function to Average

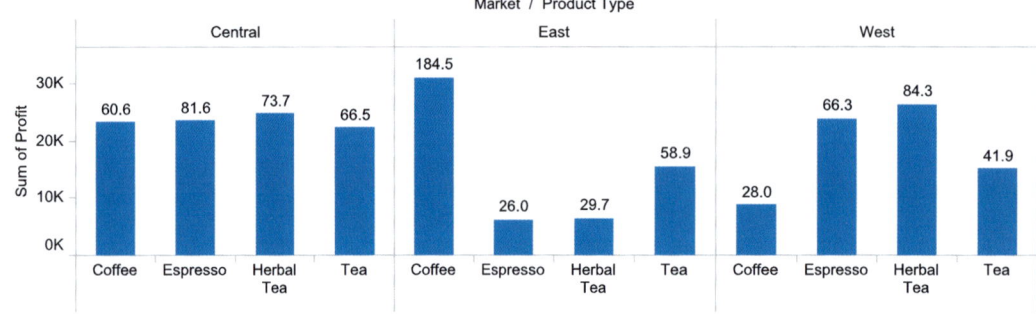

2. <u>**Color**</u>: this gives you the ability to highlight the view with a range or spectrum of colors for measure items or discrete colors for categorical dimension items. **Add *Market Size* to the Color shelf.** The default colors are assigned from the "Tableau 10" color palette, which is too dark to easily see the text on the bars. To correct this, **double-click on one of the colors in the color legend**. The Edit Colors dialog appears. **Click on the dropdown in the upper right of the dialog to change the Color Palette from "Tableau 10" to "Tableau 10 Light", then click the Assign Palette button and OK.** The view shows *Profit* for each *Market* and *Product Type* with *Market Size* color-encoded.

Modifying the view by placing *Market Size* on the Color shelf

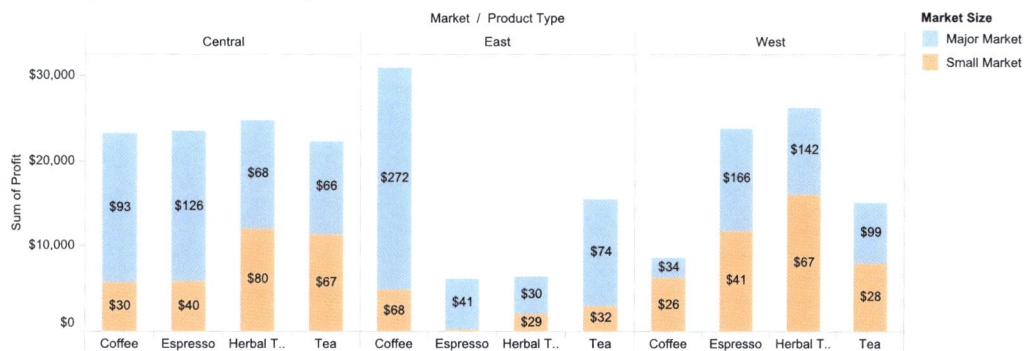

Next, **click on the down carat next to Dimensions in the Data Items area and select Create Calculated Field from the menu. Name the field "Profit vs. Budget Profit". Enter the formula *Profit - Budget Profit* by selecting the two separate measures from the Fields box and adding a minus sign between them. Move this new calculated item to the color shelf.** This will replace *Market Size*.

Creating and color encoding a new calculated field, *Profit vs. Budget Profit*

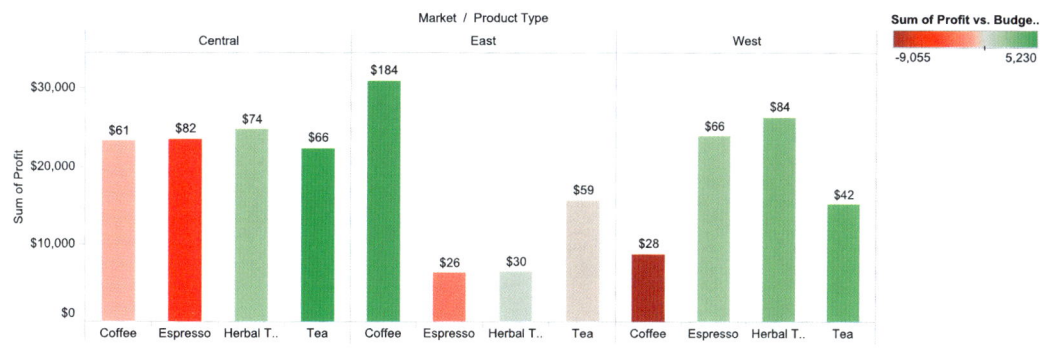

3. *Size*: allows you to alter the size of objects based on the range of values for the selected item. **Place *Sales* on the Size shelf.** Note that the widths of the bars change, notably for Espresso, Herbal Tea and Tea in the East market.

Modifying the view by placing *Sales* on the Size shelf

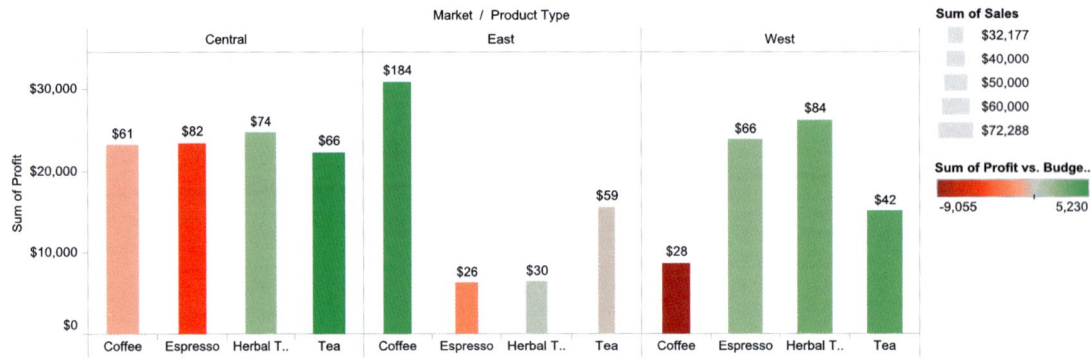

4. <u>*Shape*</u>: you can use this shelf to control the shapes that display the data from a categorical dimension item. **Click on Show Me! and select Scatter (Matrix)- graph.** This view type displays all measures in the matrix with *Product Type* color-encoded and *Market* shape-encoded.

Modifying the view in two clicks, changing the prior page via Show Me!

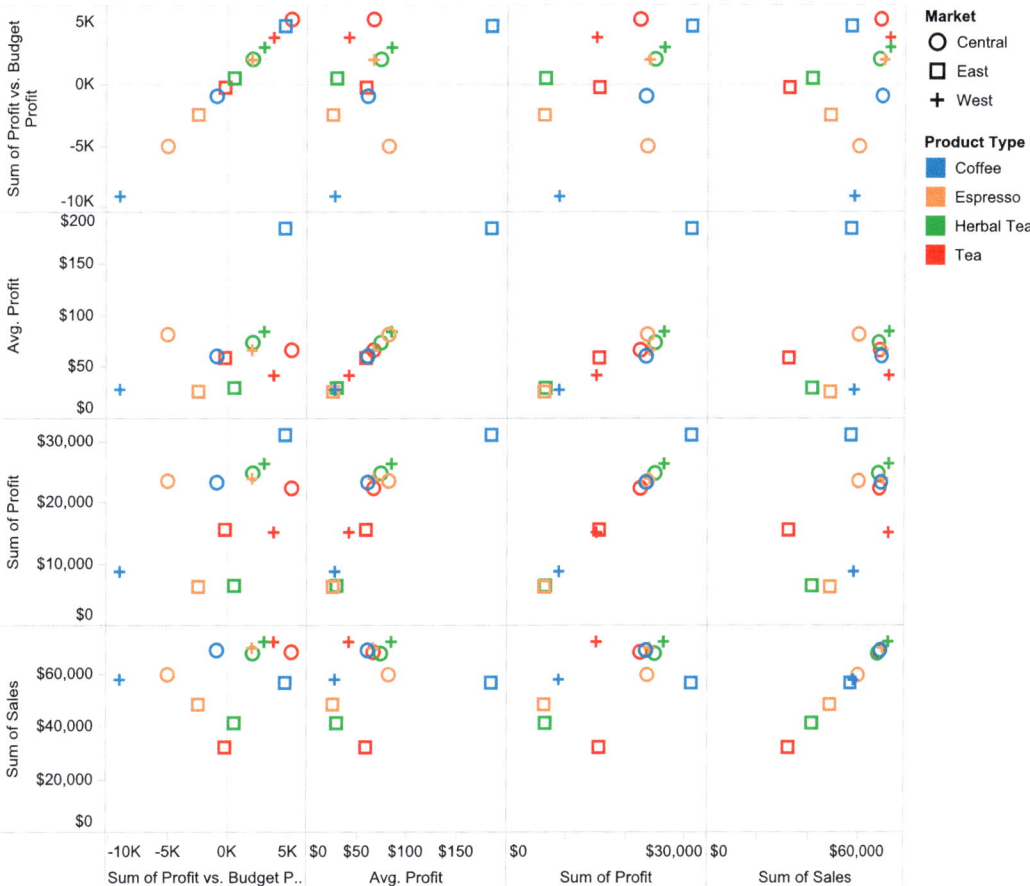

A fascinating view that allows the exploration of many questions. One step a product manager may take is to highlight all coffee products in the scatter matrix to explore how coffee is performing relative to tea for these metrics. **From the Color legend, hold down the <Ctrl> key and click on Coffee and then Espresso, right-click and select Highlight Selected Items**. The items are now highlighted in the graph and all other items are grayed out, enabling easy comparison of coffee and espresso products against tea and herbal tea.

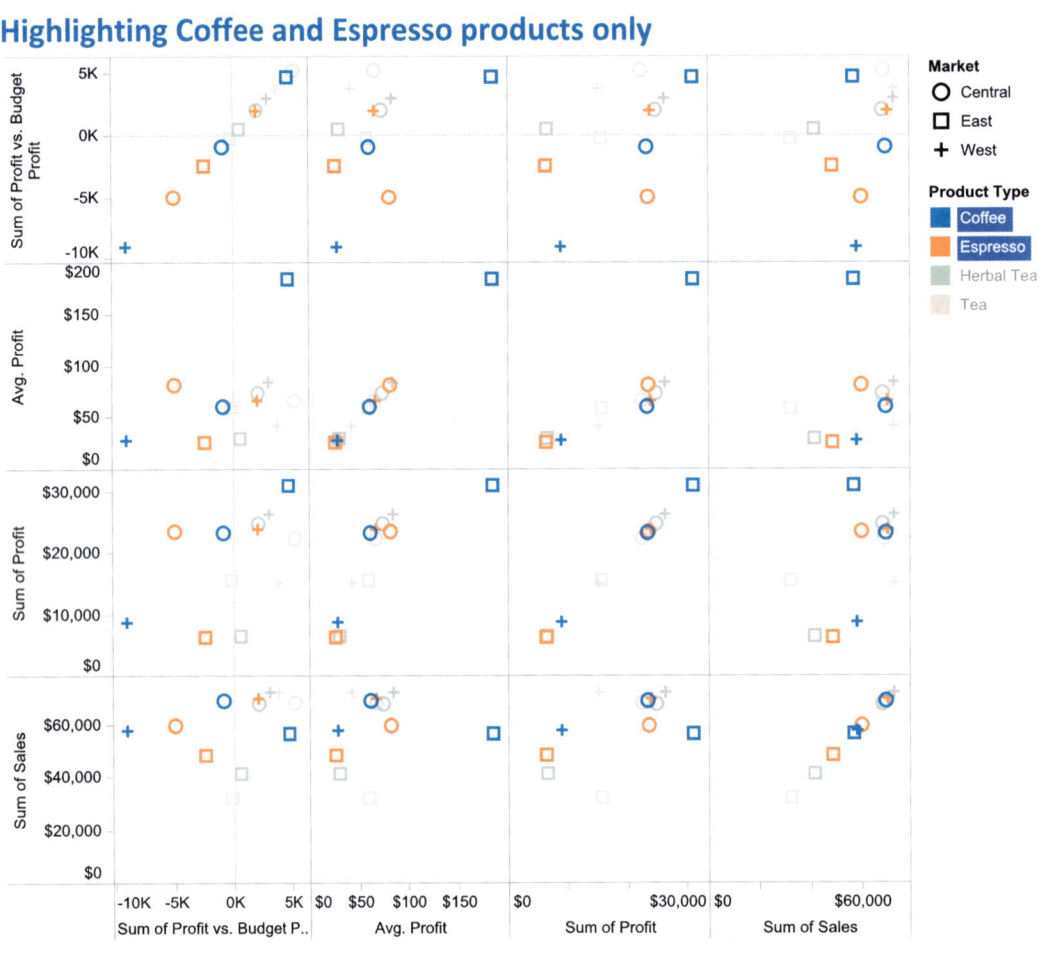

5. *Level of Detail*: the level of detail shelf controls the level at which data is summarized in your view. Using dimensional data items, the level of detail allows you to show more detail in your view without additional color or shape encoding. This is different from filtering, as it does not exclude data from the view, it simply divides or collapses data into sections to display in your view.

Remove all of the items from the Columns shelf except *Sum(Sales)* **and all items from the Rows shelf except** *Sum(Profit)*. **Also, remove** *Market* **from the Shape shelf.** The graph will now have four data points. **Add** *Product* **to the Level of Detail shelf.** The data points show each product type (color-encoded) at the product level of detail, so there are now thirteen marks. The example below also shows the same chart at the *Area Code* level of detail. Finally, to show the greatest amount of detail, **turn off all aggregation via Analysis -> Aggregate Measures**. Note that once you turn off this option, the Columns and Rows items along with the axis titles removed the aggregate functions from their names, since no aggregation is occurring!

Modify the view by placing *Product* on the Level of Detail shelf

Even more detail, place *Area Code* on the Level of Detail shelf

Modify the view by turning off aggregation and resizing the points

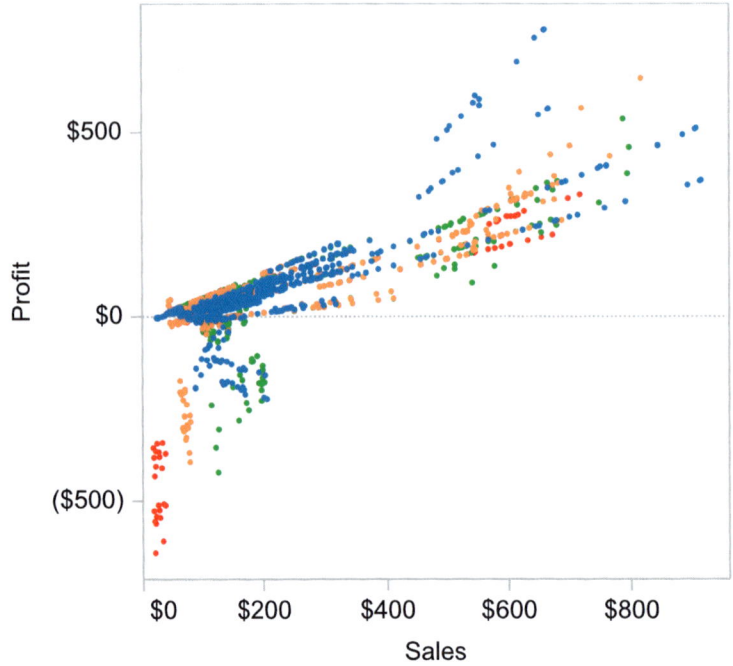

The Summary Card- rapid data insights

The Summary Card describes the measures currently shown in the view. If you have data items on the Pages and/or Filters shelves, the Summary Card will show only the data included in the current view. Five summary statistics are listed- Count, Sum, Average, Minimum, and Maximum. **Turn this on from the main menu by View -> Summary.** To copy the summary card values to the clipboard, **click on the drop down arrow from the card and select Copy to Clipboard.**

Summary Card of all measures in a view

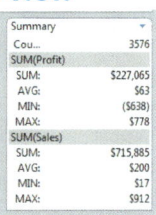

If you would like to summarize certain data points in the view, such as the data in the upper right part of the graph, you can update the Summary Card by selecting the data within the view itself. **Hold the left mouse button down and drag your mouse pointer across the data point region that you want to highlight.** The Summary Card automatically updates the statistics based on the current selection.

Summary Card of measures for upper right part of graph, note that only the bolded points in the graph are used in the summary

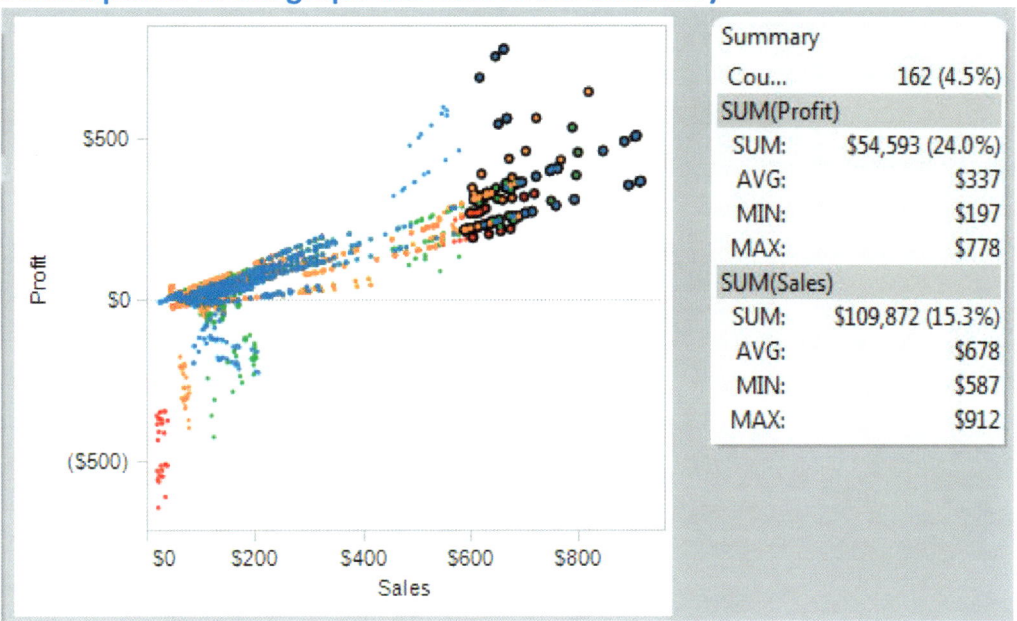

Headers and Axes

Headers and axes are automatically created by Tableau whenever items are placed on the Columns or Rows shelves. By default, a measure is represented by an axis with continuous values and a dimension is represented by a discrete or categorical header. **Please reset your view to the default layout found at the beginning of this chapter by selecting** *Market*, *Product Type* **and** *Profit*, **click Show Me!, and then click OK.** The figure shows *Sum of Profit* (a measure) as a continuous axis and *Market* and *Product Type* (dimensions) as headers.

Sum of Profit (measure) as a continuous axis and *Market* and *Product Types* (dimensions) as headers

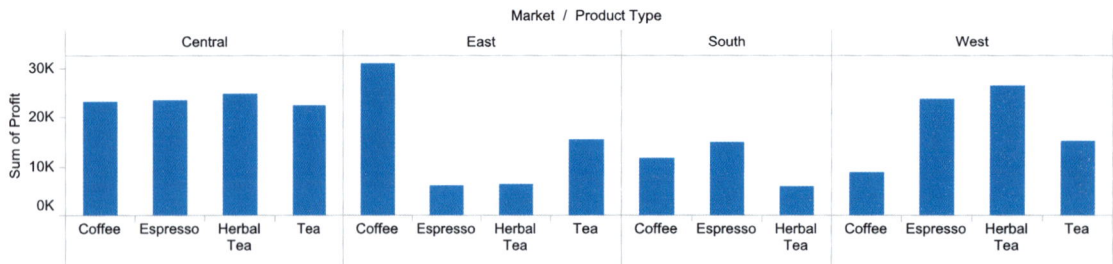

Tableau offers significant control over formatting of axis scales (formatting and appearance of the header and number fonts, orientation, etc. will be covered later in this chapter). **Click on the vertical or y-axis labeled** *Sum of Profit*, **then <Right-Click> and select Edit Axis.** The Edit Axis dialog appears, as shown in the figure below. Here you can change overall axis range, axis ranges across header groups in columns or rows, scale reversal or logarithmic scaling and tick mark formatting. You also can rename the axis by typing the new names in the title and subtitle fields. **Change the range by selecting Fixed and entering 0 in the Start field and 40,000 in the End field. Change the title to "2 Year Total Profits", and click OK to apply the changes and close the dialog.**

Edit Axis dialog box

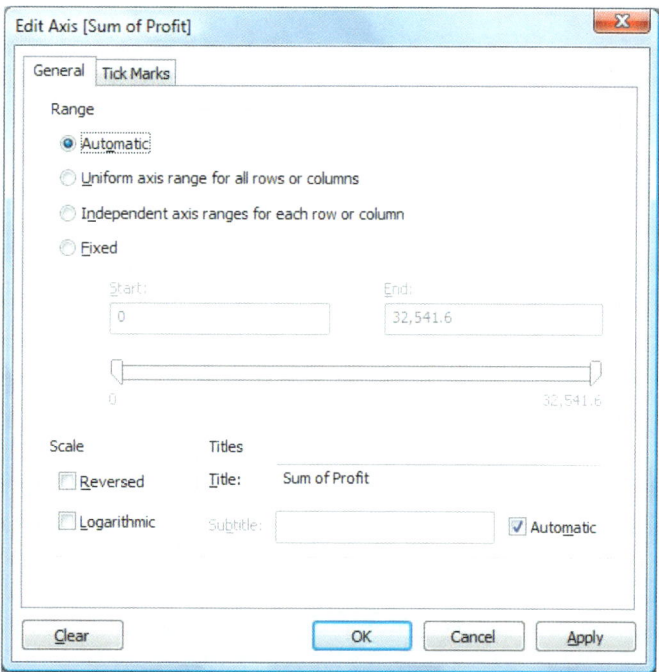

You can modify the headers in a similar manner. Click on a header value for ***Product Type*** (Espresso for example), right-click and you will see four options related to the header: Format…, Rotate Label, Show Header and Edit Alias. Format allows control over the appearance of the header text and is covered later in this chapter. Rotate Label will rotate the header labels 90 degrees counterclockwise, changing the orientation of the text from horizontal to vertical or vice versa. Show Header controls whether or not the header text is displayed for the view. Edit Alias allows you to give particular values within categorical dimensions new labels to use as headers in the view.

Right-click on the *Product Type* header and select Edit Aliases. The Edit Aliases dialog appears as shown in the figure below. **Change the Value (Alias) for Herbal Tea to Decaf Tea then click OK.** The view updates (shown below).

Renaming the alias of the header in the Edit Aliases dialog box

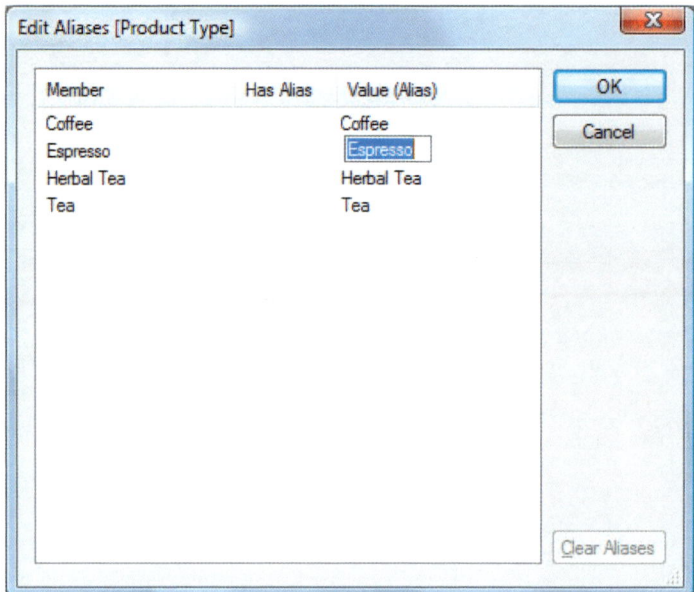

Modified title on the vertical axis and header alias in the horizontal axis

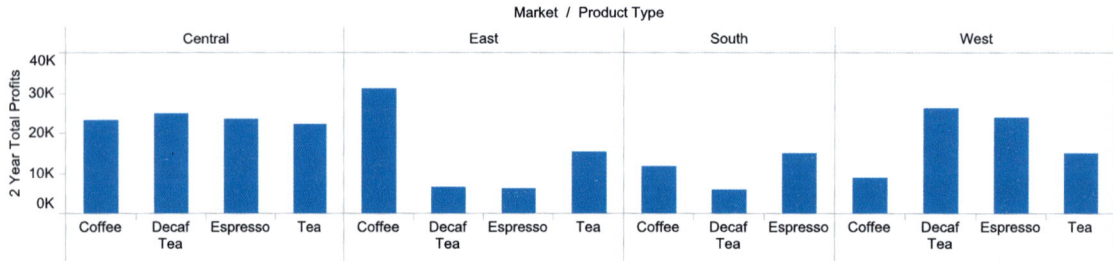

Titles, Captions, Field Labels and Legends

Titles enable quick identification of the content and purpose of your view. The Title is the same as the worksheet name. **Modify the title by selecting View -> Title on the main menu or by right-clicking on the worksheet name at the bottom of Tableau and selecting Rename Sheet, then type in Stephen.**

Captions typically present more detail about the contents of the view than the Title. Tableau automatically creates a caption based on the view layout, but you can manually modify it. **Select View -> Caption on the main menu to place the Caption card in the view. Right-click on the caption or click on the down carat at the right of the Caption card to edit the caption.** In this case, do not change anything so that the default caption will be displayed.

Field labels are the dimension items used to create the headers and are automatically displayed with the headers. For example, in the previous figure in the Header and Axes section, the field label is "*Market* / *Product Type*". In this case, you can hide the field labels by **right-clicking on them and selecting Hide Field Label for Columns.**

Legends are used when data values are encoded by color, shape and/or size providing the keys the understand the encoding. In Tableau, each legend can be customized individually.

To follow the example, first code the following data items: **place *Market Size* on the Color shelf, change the value in the Marks dropdown from Automatic to Shape, place *Marketing* on the Size shelf, and *Market Size* on the Shape selector on the Marks shelf. Simply click on the down carat on any individual Legend shelf and select Edit Colors, Sizes, etc.**

Changing the title, adding an automatic caption as a view footnote, hiding the field labels, and customizing size/shape/color legends

Formatting values in your Views

Tableau is extremely flexible and allows you to format all elements in the view. **Right-click on any element in the view and select Format**. The Format dialog appears in place of the Data Items window on the far left of the screen.

The Format dialog stays visible **until you close it by clicking on the x in the upper right corner of the dialog**. Within the Format dialog, the options vary based on your selected item. For example, in the figure below, the Format dialog on the left side is entitled "Format Product Type". **Click on one of the icons at the top of the format dialog or click on a different item in the view so another element of the view can be edited.** The right side of the figure is the Format Shading dialog.

Examples of Format dialog boxes

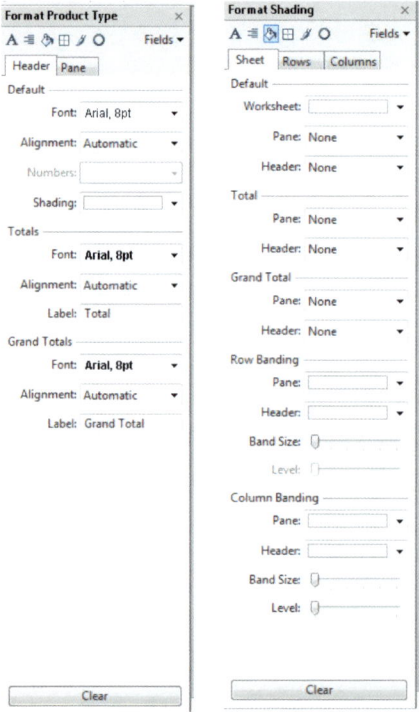

The symbols across the top of the Format dialog represent the various elements that can be formatted. From left to right, the symbols are Font, Alignment, Shading, Borders, Lines, Marks and a dropdown menu for the Fields that you are currently using in your view. Formatting of Font, Alignment, Shading, Borders and Lines can be performed at the overall Sheet, Rows or Columns level. Marks can be formatted only at the overall Sheet level. Formatting can be copied from one sheet to another – even across workbooks.

It is easy to format the text of the headers and axes to reproduce the next figure. **Right-click on the vertical axis (2 Year Total Profits) and select Format.** The Format dialog appears. **In the Font field, select tan from the color palette.** This changes the font color. **Using the Fields dropdown menu, change the data item to Product Type. In the Font field, select tan from the color palette and select the italic box to italicize the text.**

Formatting text of headers and axes

Page intentionally left blank for proper book pagination.

Chapter 7

Organizing the data in your Views- Sorting, Filtering, Quick Calculations, Spotlighting and View Trending

_____

Chapter Highlights

- Sorting your views for clarity

- Filtering your views to find the right information

- Aggregating measures- sums, averages and more

- Use percentages to find the right ratios

- Quick table calculations- complex calculations made easy

- Spotlighting your view to call out key information

- Totals and subtotals

- Use Trend Lines to model your data

_____

This chapter will cover many of the features in Tableau that control how the data appear in your view once you have added the desired items to the shelves. This includes arranging your view, hiding irrelevant or confusing information, adjusting how measures are calculated, enabling the use of percentages to understand parts of the whole or ratios, easy calculations that can radically change your understanding of the data, spotlighting or calling out certain values, adding subtotals and totals to your view and using trend lines to summarize overall data patterns.

This chapter covers a lot of material in-depth, so you might need more time than other chapters to be comfortable with this content. Enjoy!

Simple and advanced Sorting of Views

Tableau automatically sorts your data along dimensional items used in your view. By default, it sorts the category labels in ascending alphabetical order. For example, Tea, Coffee and Espresso are sorted as Coffee, Espresso and Tea.

It may be useful to sort your view by the measure in use. The quickest way to sort by the measure is **to click on the Sort ascending or Sort descending buttons on the Tableau toolbar**, shown in the figure below.

Sort ascending and Sort descending buttons on the toolbar

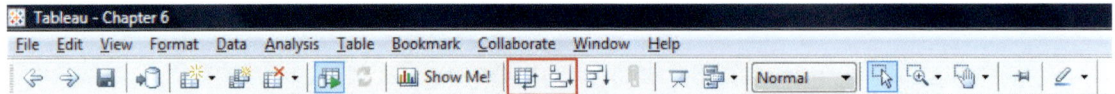

For example, you may want to sort your market regions so that they are ordered in the view from highest to lowest profit. **Please reset your view to the default layout used in Chapter 6 by selecting *Market*, *Product Type* and *Profit*, and click Show Me! and OK.** To obtain the view on the left in the figure, **remove *Product Type* from the Columns shelf.** To see the view on the right, click **on the Sort descending button.** The Sort buttons are quite powerful, as they use the inputs from your selection to infer the type of sort that you want.

Aligned bar views with *Profit* by *Market*:

left view-unsorted, right view- sorted via the Sort descending toolbar item

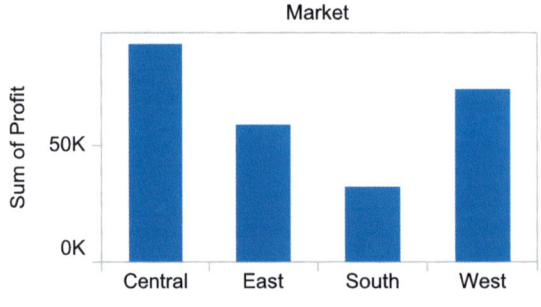

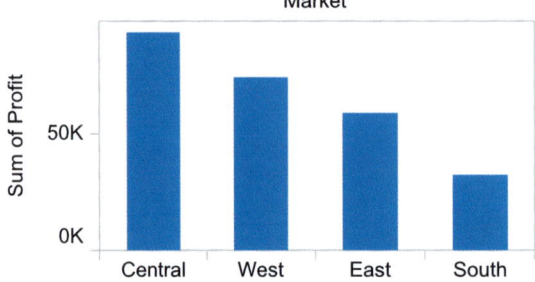

A variety of advanced sorting methods is available beyond the default alphabetic by dimension and the sort ascending and descending toolbar items by measure. **Right-click on a dimensional item on the Column or Rows shelf and select Sort.** The Sort dialog box will appear as shown in the next figure.

Sort dialog box

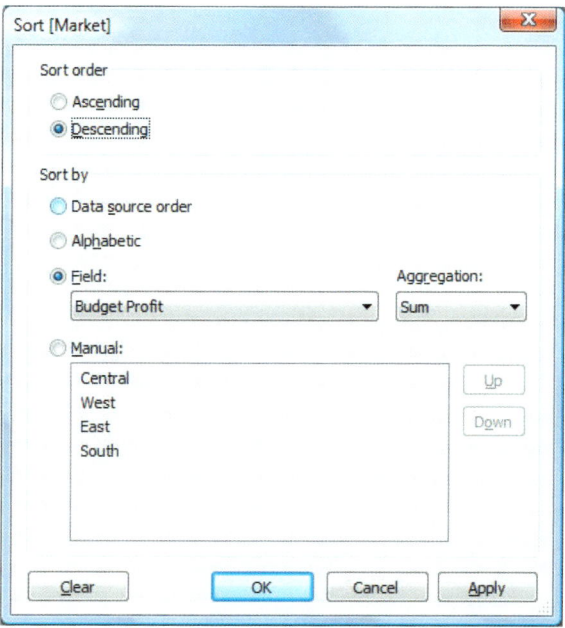

! *Alternate Route*: You can drag and drop items in legends or rows and columns to manually sort them.

From the Sort dialog, you can sort data by the order of the original data source, alphabetically, by any field in your data source, or manually for custom sorting. At the top of the dialog, you can specify either Ascending or Descending order, applicable for alphabetic and field sort options. **In this example, select Descending order, Sort by Field-> *Sales* and click OK** to yield the figure below. If you are unable to do this because the Sort order field is grayed out, **select Field-> *Sales* first, which will then allow you to select Descending under Sort order.** Note that this results in a different order than descending profit, which is surprising since you would typically expect a strong relationship between sales and profit.

Using the Sort dialog box to Sort by Field

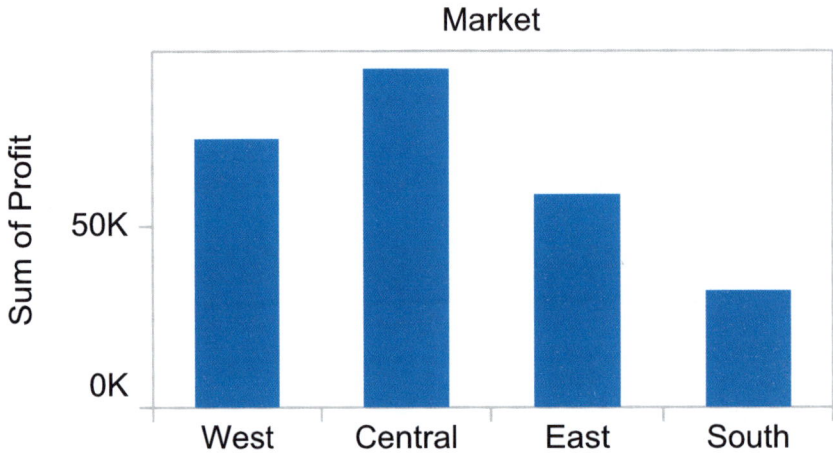

Although you will need to keep *Sales* sorted for the next example, in general all sorting can be cleared by **right-clicking on the dimension item in the Columns or Rows shelf and selecting Clear Sort.**

! *Performance Tip*: The major difference between the one-click Sort buttons and the Sort dialog is that one-click is 'one time' and does not automatically update as the data or view updates. The dialog computes the sort every time the view is updated.

Simple and advanced Filtering of Views

Filters reduce the data that are displayed in your view by allowing you to select a subset of the data. Filters can be specified using dimension or measure items, although the two types have different dialogs and options.

The simplest filter uses the labels of dimension items or marks in the view. To filter by dimension item, **click on a label or multiple labels and right-click, selecting either Keep Only or Exclude.** Both options will create a filter on the dimension item, keeping or excluding the selected items.

Filtering of dimension items is also available by dragging the item from the Dimensions pane to the Filter shelf. For example, **drag *State* from the Dimensions pane to the Filter shelf**. The Filter dialog appears, as shown in the figure below. There are three tabs available: General, Condition, and Top. The General tab (displayed in the figure) allows selection of the filter criteria by label. To follow this example, **select California, Florida and Illinois, and then click OK.**

Filter dialog box with General tab displayed and resulting view

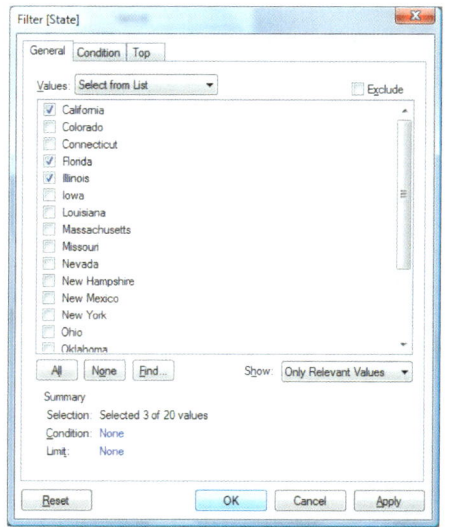
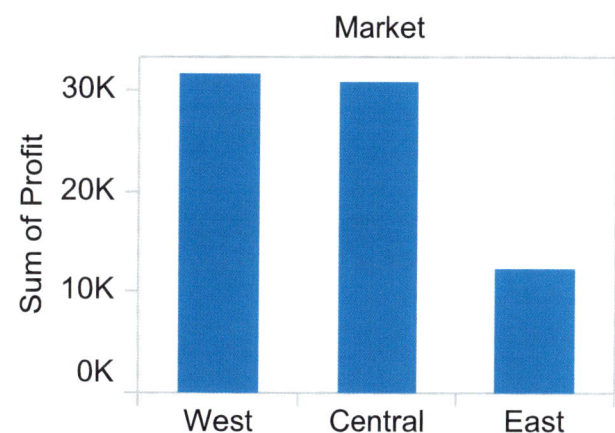

The Condition tab allows filtering the view using any data field with an aggregate function condition such as Sum, Average and Count (aggregations will be discussed in detail in the next section). **Using the down carat next to *State* on the Filter shelf, pull down the Filter menu and select Filter->Condition tab, choose By Field->*Sales*->Sum->greater than (>), enter 60,000 and click OK.** This is shown in the next figure.

Filter dialog box with Condition tab displayed and resulting view

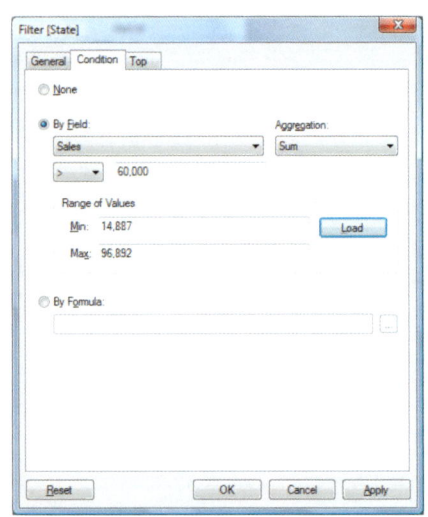
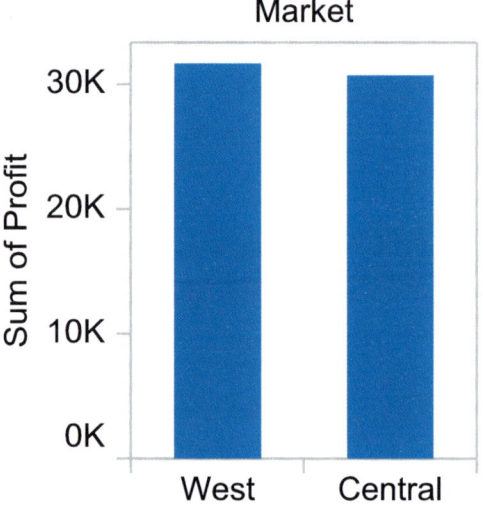

The Top tab allows you to filter the view using the top or bottom rankings of any data field with an aggregate function condition, such as the ten states with the lowest sales. **To do this, pull down the Filter menu by clicking on the down carat next to *State* on the Filter shelf. Choose the Top tab->By Field->Bottom->10->*Sales*->Average.** This is shown in the next figure.

Filter dialog box with Top tab displayed and resulting view

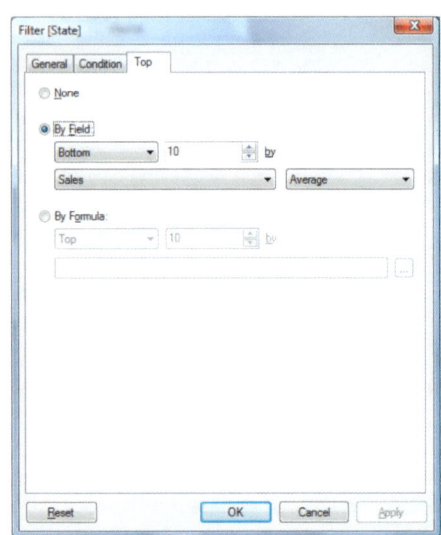
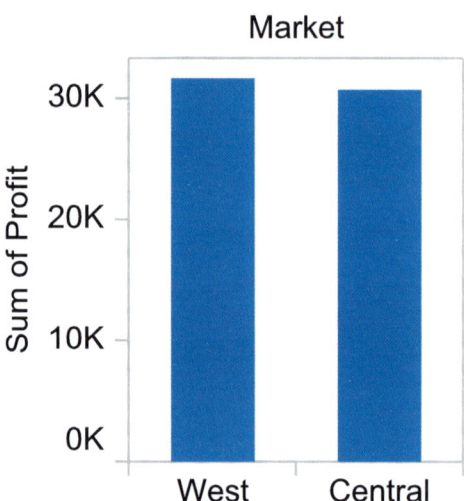

! *Performance Tip*: A dimension filter is applied independently of all the other filters, so the condition and top elements will not consider other filters in play unless you add those other filters to the context.

Aggregations for measures- specify the right summaries

Tableau automatically assigns an aggregate function to all items that are measures. By default, the aggregate function for non-geographic measures is to Sum the data. Each cell or value used to create the view is included when Tableau calculates aggregates. Other common aggregations include Average and Count. Average is similar to the mean of all the records in a cell and Count is the number of records available in the data source for the cell. Less commonly used aggregations include Minimum, Maximum, Standard Deviation, Standard Deviation (Population), Variance, and Variance (Population).

You can change the default aggregation from the measures part of the Data shelf **by right-clicking on the item and selecting Set Default -> Aggregation.** Once a measure item is added to the view, you can also customize the aggregation for the current view. **On the Column or Row shelf, click on the down carat in the oval of the measure item. Select Measure and the desired aggregation function.**

 To follow this example, **please reset your view once again to the default layout by selecting** *Market*, *Product Type* **and** *Profit*, **and clicking Show Me! and OK.**

Add *Profit* to the Rows shelf of the view two more times. On the Rows shelf, change the aggregate of the second Profit item to Average and the third Profit item to Maximum. The figure below shows the result- the three aggregations are displayed in separate rows. By applying multiple aggregations to the same measure, you can gain additional insights compared to having only a single aggregation view.

Applying three aggregations to the same measure item, *Profit*

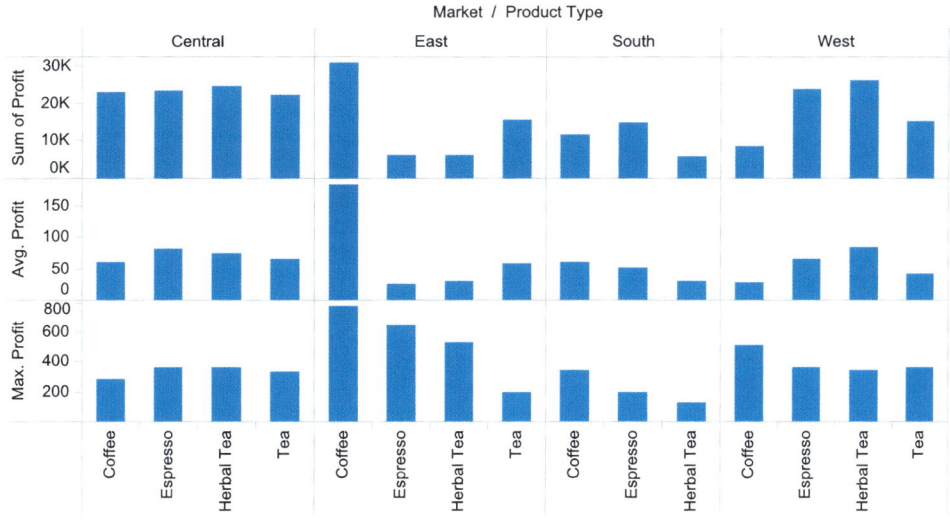

Percentages provide balance to compare ratios

Using percentages in Tableau is easy and informative. Percentages allow the rapid comparison of cells across columns and/or rows when the total amounts vary widely across cells. Percentages can be calculated as a percentage of all values, a percentage of values in a row or column, and a percentage of values in a cell. Other less common percentage calculations are also available.

Please reset your view to the default layout by selecting *Market*, *Product Type* and *Profit*, and clicking Show Me! and OK. Add *Market Size* to the beginning of the rows shelf before *Sum (Profit)*. The profit for each product type in each region and market size is shown in the view (not pictured here).

Perhaps you are more interested in understanding the relative contribution of each product type to a region/market size. Since various panes where *Region* and *Market Size* intersect have different total profits, it is hard to gauge the relative contribution of each product type to a pane. To simplify this comparison, **from the main menu select Analysis -> Percentage of-> Pane.** This will change the metric calculation from Sum of Profit to percentage of Total Sum of Profit for a pane, as shown below.

You will notice that in the original view, overall profits in the South were much lower than the other regions. Once the view was adjusted to show the percentage of profit within each pane, this profit level is adjusted based on the total profit in each pane with each pane totaling 100%. This is very useful if you want to highlight the relative profit contribution of each product in a market.

Percentage of Total Sum of Profit for each Product Type, by Region and Market Size

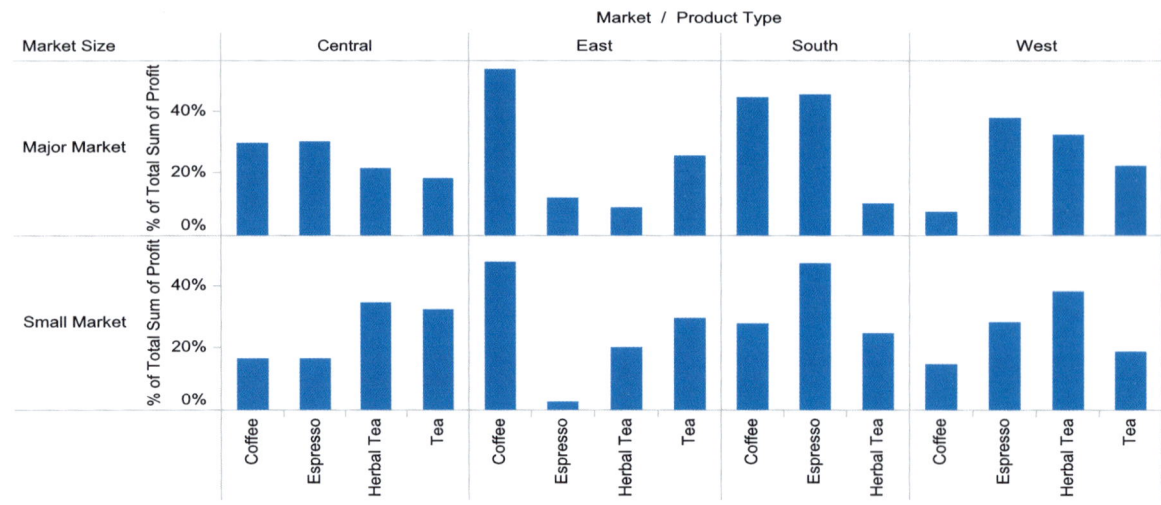

Quick Table Calculations

Quick Table Calculations are often related to date views and are applied to measures used in the view. Examples of Quick Table Calculations include Running Total, Difference (versus prior period or cell), Percent Difference (versus prior period or cell), Percent of Total, Moving Average (smoothes out data that varies widely by time period), Year-to-Date Total (called YTD Total in Tableau), Compound Growth Rate, Year-over-Year Growth rate, Year-to-Date Growth (called YTD Growth in Tableau, and defined as cumulative YTD growth in measure over prior year.)

The example shown can be created by **selecting** *Date* and *Profit* **from the Coffee Chain dataset. Click Show Me! and select the default selection- Line (Discrete). Drill-down on the** *Date* **variable twice, from** *Year* **to** *Quarter* **and from** *Quarter* **to** *Month*. **This can be done by clicking on the plus sign next to the** *Date* **item on the Columns shelf.**

Add *Profit* **to the Rows shelf one more time. Also add** *Sales* **to the Rows shelf. For the second** *Profit* **item on the Rows shelf, click on the down carat and select Quick Table Calculation -> YTD Total. For** *Sales* **on the Rows shelf, click on the down carat and select Quick Table Calculation -> YTD Total. Drag the** *Year(Date)* **item from the Columns shelf to the Color selector on the Marks shelf.**

Quick Table Calculations- YTD Totals for *Date* and *Profit* with *Year* in color

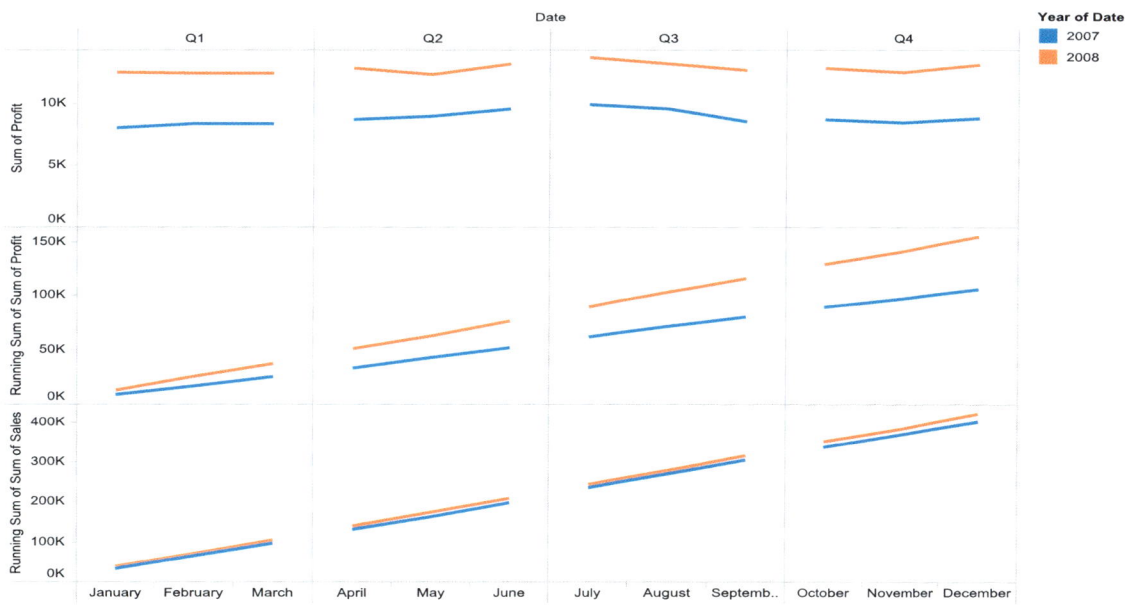

The Running Sums of *Profit* and *Sales* contrast quite dramatically. You can immediately observe very little difference in 2007 and 2008 sales growth through the year but substantially greater profit growth in 2008 over 2007. YTD running totals can help with estimating final sales and profit figures based on prior year patterns and current year trajectory.

Spotlighting your View to call out important values

Spotlighting is a powerful feature in Tableau used to highlight measure values in a table or chart that meet criteria defined by you, typically by color encoding. For example, you may want to highlight products that have profits above $10,000 or below $3,000 to emphasize that they require additional discussion and research. Using spotlighting, you can make these products "jump" off the page.

To follow this example, **reset your view to the default layout by selecting *Market*, *Product Type* and *Profit*, and click Show Me! and OK. Then, move *Market* from the Columns shelf to the Rows shelf and add *Product* to the end of the Columns shelf. From the Data Items / Measures pane, right-click on *Profit* and select Create Calculated Field.** The Calculated Field dialog appears. **Change the name of the Calculated Field to "Profit Spotlight" and enter the Formula as:**

IF SUM([Profit]) >= 10000 THEN "Best"
ELSEIF SUM([Profit]) <= 3000 THEN "Worst" (Note that the "ELSEIF" function is one word.)
ELSE "Middle of the Pack" END

Click on the Check Formula button below the formula. The dialog should confirm it is a valid calculation, but if an error message pops up, check your formula for typos. **Click OK. *Profit Spotlight***, the calculated item, will appear in the Data Items / Measures pane. **Double-click on the item and it is automatically added to the Color selector of the Marks shelf.**

A color legend card appears. **Double-click on the Best color.** The Edit Colors dialog appears. **Change Best to green, Middle of the Pack to gray, and Worst to red, and then click OK. Right-click on South and West in the view and select Exclude.** Only Central and East will be displayed in the view.

Spotlighting Products with the Best and Worst Profits by color encoding (only Central and East markets shown)

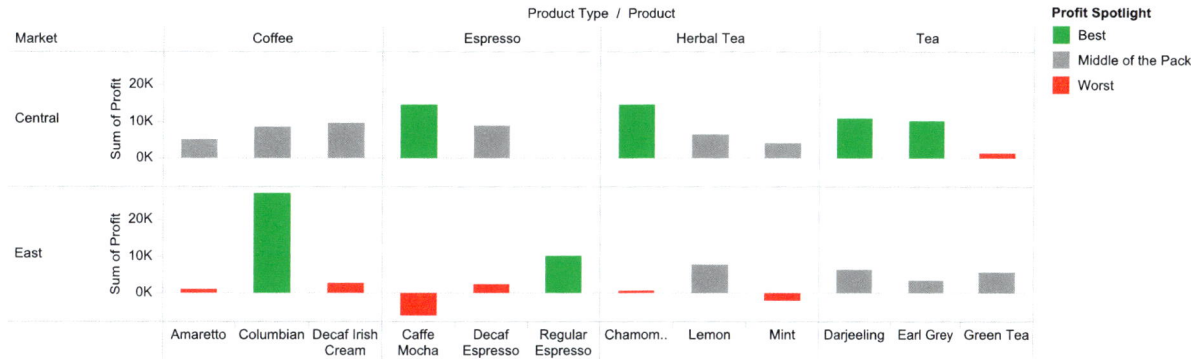

In this case, spotlighting makes it easy to see that Central has only one underperforming product, the products with the highest profits are different between Central and East, and East has many more underperforming products but also has the highest profit product.

! *Alternate Route*: This is a simple example that also can be done by using the Create Calculated Field function. Editing the default color range can give the same effect with less effort than the calculation.

! *Performance Tip*: The advantage of using Spotlighting over the Create Calculated Field function is that values of interest that do not appear in your current dataset but that may appear in future datasets will be spotlighted automatically in the manner that you select.

Totals and Subtotals to sum up parts of yourVview

Subtotals and Totals give you the powerful ability to summarize your view at the view pane level (the crossing of categorical item values used in the view) or as a grand total or totals for rows and/or columns. Due to the nature of subtotals, they are available only if there are at least two dimensional items in either the Rows or Columns shelf.

Although the function includes the word "total", Tableau does not simply add up all the values - it uses the aggregation specified for the measures in your view. Therefore, totals for summed measures would be the sum of the sums in each cell, but the total for averaged measures would be the average of the underlying data values used in the cells.

Some words of caution: if you are using a pre-summarized data source for your view and an aggregate function other than Count or Sum, Tableau could return wrong values for subtotals or grand totals. Tableau calculates the totals based on the original data, it does not calculate the total based on the results displayed. *Also be careful to not sum percentages- these should be averaged!*

Now, you are going to build upon the example from the previous section on spotlighting. **Click on Show Me! and change the view type to Text Table (Cross-tab).** Exclude the Coffee and Tea product types from the view. **Click on Coffee, <Ctrl> and then Tea, then right-click and select Exclude. Add *Market Size* to the end of the Rows shelf. In the main menu, click on Table -> Add All Subtotals.**

Adding Subtotals to a spotlighted Text Table

| Market | Market Size | Espresso | | | | Herbal Tea | | | |
		Caffe Mocha	Decaf Espresso	Regular Espresso	Total	Chamo..	Lemon	Mint	Total
Central	Major Market	11,457	6,154		17,611	6,439	2,083	4,069	12,591
	Small Market	3,185	2,705		5,890	7,996	4,170		12,166
	Total	14,642	8,859		23,501	14,435	6,253	4,069	24,757
East	Major Market	-6,069	1,738	10,274	5,943	764	6,955	-3,369	4,350
	Small Market	-163	673	-209	301		947	1,126	2,073
	Total	-6,232	2,411	10,065	6,244	764	7,902	-2,243	6,423

Profit Spotlight
- 🟩 Best
- ⬜ Middle of the Pack
- 🟥 Worst

Note that profits from all products and market sizes have been summed in the table. However, grand totals are not shown, which would summarize across all markets or across all product types. Turn off Subtotals by **choosing Table -> Remove All Subtotals from the main menu.** Turn on Grand Totals for both Rows and Columns: **Select Table -> Row Grand Totals and Table -> Column Grand Totals.**

Adding Grand Totals to a spotlighted Text Table

| Market | Market Size | Espresso | | | Herbal Tea | | | Grand Total |
		Caffe Mocha	Decaf Espresso	Regular Espresso	Chamo..	Lemon	Mint	
Central	Major Market	11,457	6,154		6,439	2,083	4,069	30,202
	Small Market	3,185	2,705		7,996	4,170		18,056
East	Major Market	-6,069	1,738	10,274	764	6,955	-3,369	10,293
	Small Market	-163	673	-209		947	1,126	2,374
Grand Total		8,410	11,270	10,065	15,199	14,155	1,826	60,925

Profit Spotlight
- 🟩 Best
- ⬜ Middle of the Pack
- 🟥 Worst

In general, subtotals and grand totals are less useful when using bar or line chart views. Often, the totals greatly surpass the individual values, resetting the values on the axis labels and making the chart difficult to read. Totals are often more useful and easier to include on histograms, pie charts, and maps, or aggregations other than Sum and Count, such as Average, Minimum and Maximum.

Model your data with Trend Lines

Tableau has the capability to model your data with a trend line to help you visualize the overall patterns of the data. The trend line can be based on a linear, logarithmic, or polynomial regression model. Additionally, the trend can be adjusted across dimensional levels so that each pane has a fitted line for the data displayed in that pane. For Tableau to ensure that the math for the trend line is valid, the data items that are on your horizontal and vertical axes need to be equally spaced or have the ability to be converted into a range of continuous values. This includes continuous dimension items, measures added as dimensions, and date dimension items.

Tableau can use trend lines to report significance levels between two variables based on a regression model. Since statistical significance is a complex topic, it will not be described in detail here. One simple way to explain significance is with a p-value, which indicates how well the model fits your data. Lower p-values are better, with values less than 0.05 typically considered "statistically significant", usually written as $p<0.05$. For example, a p-value of 0.03 tells you that there is a 3% chance that the trend line fitting your data values is describing a relationship between your two variables that is random or does not actually exist (i.e., 3% chance that there is no true pattern and the relationship is just noise). Or stated another way, the probability is that three times out of one-hundred, the relationship described by the trend line doesn't actually exist, while ninety-seven times out of one-hundred, it probably does exist. In Tableau, p-values are available for the entire model, a particular line in a pane, and specific data items used to explain the relationship between your numeric variables.

For example, you may want to try to estimate profit from sales. Start with a new, **empty worksheet by selecting Edit-> New Worksheet on the main menu (or<Ctrl>- M) and do not return to the default view for this chapter. Add *Profit* to the Rows shelf.** Note that the item you want to "predict" should be on the vertical or Y-axis, which corresponds to the Rows shelf. **Next, add *Sales* to the Columns shelf.** Turn off the aggregation of data to use all data points in the Trend Line model, **select Analysis -> Aggregate Measures. Reduce the size of the data points to the smallest setting by moving the Size slider on the Marks card all to the way to the left.**

Scatter Graph of *Profit* vs. *Sales*

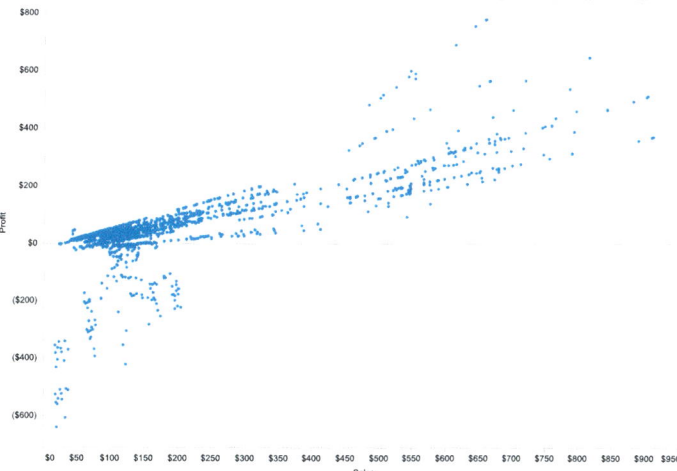

Add a trend line to the view by **right-clicking on the Scatter graph and selecting Trend Lines.**
The trend line appears with the default linear (straight) form. To describe the fit of the trend
line, **right-click on the Scatter graph again and select Describe Trend Model and** the Describe
Trend Model dialog box appears (which you can copy to a clipboard).

Scatter Graph of *Profit* vs. *Sales* with Trend Line and Describe Trend Model dialog box

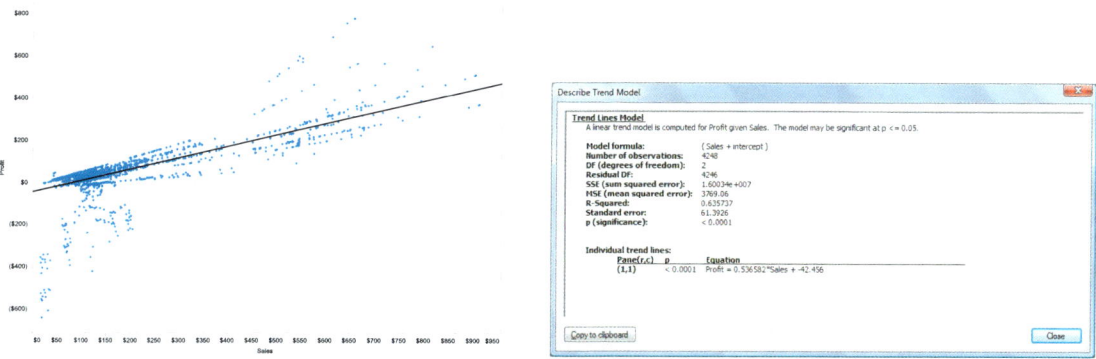

Note that the trend line appears to be drawn across the middle of the data points with some
data point outliers towards the bottom left and upper right. While there is a noticeable band of
data points near the line, you can see that although the linear trend line does not perfectly fit
the relationship between *Profit* and *Sales*, it is a good description. Note that the Describe Trend
Model box shows a significant p-value of < 0.0001. It also shows another very valuable statistic
called the R-Squared, which attempts to estimate how much of the data variability is actually
explained by the model. In this case, 0.638, or 63.8% of the variability in the data values is
accounted for by using *Sales* to predict *Profit*. At the bottom of the pane, you can see the
algebraic expression of how *Sales* can be used to estimate *Profit*: multiply *Sales* by 0.537 and

subtract 42.5 to estimate *Profit*. This makes sense since you have fixed costs (the intercept, -42.5) and variable costs (you make only an additional 53.7 cents in profit for each additional dollar of sales)!

To further refine the trend line, change the type of line fit. For example, try to draw trend lines based on year and market. **Drag *Date* to the Columns shelf before *Sales* and drag *Market* to the rows shelf before *Profit* (copy). Finally, add *Product Type* to the Color selector on the Marks shelf and keep only the Central region by right-clicking on it in the view and selecting Keep Only.** The Central region is chosen since it appears to have a very strong relationship between *Sales* and *Profit*, shown by the tight grouping of the data points around the trend lines.

Modifying Trend Lines based on *Year* and *Market*

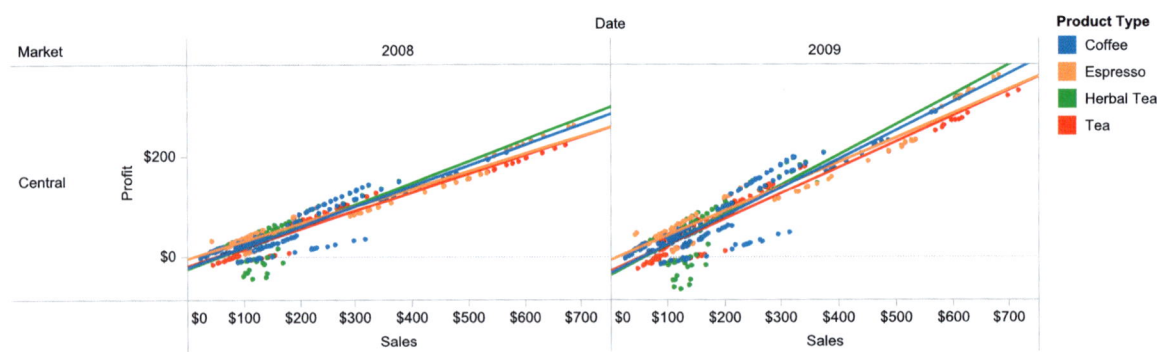

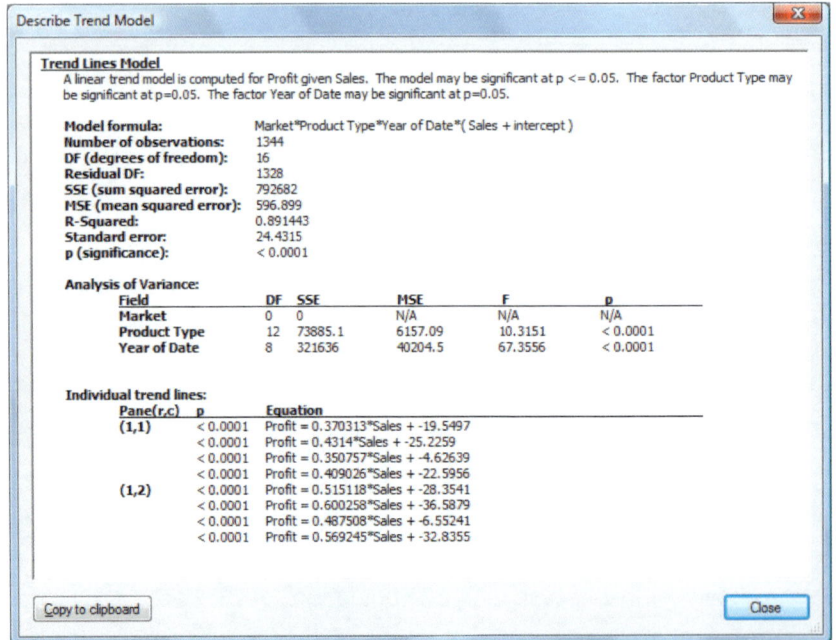

The p-value is still < 0.0001 (highly significant), but the large improvement in R-Squared from 0.638 to 0.891 is exciting. The model accounts for almost all (89.1%) of the variability in actual profit versus expected profit! In real-world business applications, it is rare to see R-Squared values above 60-80%, so this is very impressive. Examining the other fields used in the model, you can see that both *Product Type* and *Year of Date* are significant factors in explaining the model. Each *Product Type* has its own trend line and therefore a unique model describing the relationship between *Profit* and *Sales* for that *Product Type* only.

If you wanted to experiment further with the line type or other aspects of the model, **right-click on the graph and select Edit Trend Lines.** The Trend Lines Options dialog box appears. Here you can change the model type and factors included in the model. You can choose to allow a trend line per color (in this case automatically selected) instead of one trend line overall for all of the colors, or product types in this example. You also can force the y-intercept to zero.

Trend Lines Options dialog box

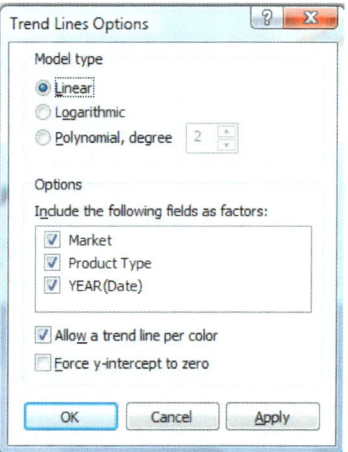

Concluding the trend line section, I will leave you with some important points to consider about trend line models and statistical analysis:

1) A model with a good fit does not necessarily imply that one variable causes changes to occur in the second variable. For example, a statistically significant model relating temperature with rainfall does not demonstrate that one causes the other to fluctuate, just that the model can describe the relationship between the two. Further knowledge of the process at hand is required to assess if one variable causes changes in the other. The model simply shows they move together.

2) A statistically significant model, indicated by the p-value, can usually be created by adding enough data points. Be sure to examine the R-Squared to see how much of the variability in the data is explained.

3) R-Squared can be skewed by adding more explanatory variables or factors to a trend line model, so try to use a reasonable number of factors to explain the relationship. In general, fewer items that have a high R-Squared are better than many items with a slightly higher R-Squared.

4) Be careful about using this type of model to forecast future values - especially if the external factors around your historic data have changed significantly!

5) If you have several factors in a model that are significant and you would like to remove some to simplify the model, first try removing the ones with the lower SSE values. SSE values measure how much of the data variability is explained by the factor, so factors with higher values for SSE are generally better to keep!

6) Be cautious about turning on the option to set the y-intercept to zero- only do this if you are certain that this condition is true for your problem at hand.

Chapter 8

Managing data is critical for awesome results-
Data Items and data management in Tableau

Chapter Highlights

- Data items

  - Names

  - Types

  - Roles

  - Properties

  - Attributes

- View Underlying Data

- Bins to group numeric data

- Grouping dimensions into categories

- The power of sets to combine and filter your views

Many people find data management intimidating and confusing, so they attempt to avoid this topic. I think Tableau has made it easy for most people to manage their data with a wide array of simple yet powerful features. This chapter is very important because effective data management is a frequently overlooked key to analytic success!

Please note that the examples in this chapter use the **Sample – Superstore Sales (Excel)** sample data source, included with the Tableau application.

Data items: names, types, roles, properties, and attributes

Item Names

Item names in Tableau are based on the names in your selected data source. Within Tableau, you can rename items to make them relevant for your audience. For example, the item name "Profit" may seem reasonable for the Marketing team but might not be a specific enough name for the Finance team, who refer to this item as "Gross Profit". Note that renaming an item has no effect on the names in the original data source.

From the Measures pane, right-click on *Profit* **and select Rename from the menu.** The Rename Field dialog appears- **change the name to** *Gross Profit* **and click OK.**

Rename Field dialog box (field refers to your data item)

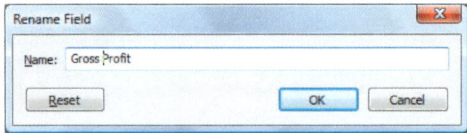

If you think an item may be irrelevant or confusing, it can be hidden from view by **right-clicking on the item and selecting Hide.** To return hidden items to the view, **click on the down carat next to Dimensions or Measures in the Data Items pane, and select Show Hidden Fields.**

Data Types

Tableau offers five types of data items: **Number**, **Date & Time**, **Date**, **String and Boolean**. By default, when Tableau connects to your data, it determines which type is the best match for a data item using the data source information and rules around data types. It is important to note that items will behave differently in your views based on the data type. Typically, you will only need to modify data types when using Access, Excel or text files as data sources. Relational and multi-dimensional databases are usually pre-formatted so that Tableau can select correct data types when you open them.

It is easy to change data types from the item context menu by **right-clicking on the item and selecting Change Data Type.** These are the rules for changing data types:
- Any data type can be converted to *String*.
- A *Number* can be converted to *Date* or *Date & Time*, but this should only be done if your number values meet date convention requirements for your data source.
- *Date* and *Date & Time* can be easily interchanged:
  - Dates simply add 00:00:00 as the time when converted to *Date & Time.*
  - *Date & Time* fields lose their time aspect if converted to *Date*.

To change the default type, **from the Dimensions pane, right-click on Zip Code, select Change Data Type from the menu and select String.**

The Change Data Type submenu

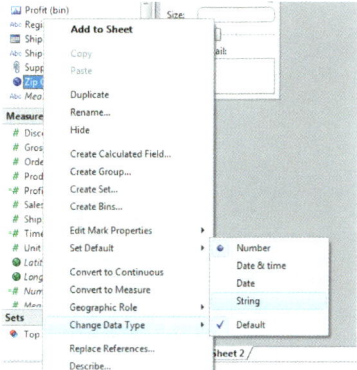

Dimensions and Measures

In Tableau, **dimensions** and **measures** are the primary means of grouping data items in the Data Items pane. By default, Tableau treats any field containing qualitative (e.g., customer type of "New", "Old", "Returning") or categorical (e.g., region of "West", "East") information as a *dimension*. In general, *dimensions* are items used to create row or column headers in a view.

Tableau automatically treats any field containing numeric information as a *measure*. *Measures* typically produce axes when added to the rows or columns shelves. *Measures* are computed using the specified aggregation for each unique combination of row and column *dimensions* used in the view. For example, the data source engine calculates **Sum of Sales** for each dimension item combination (e.g., State and Month) used in the view.

There is an important technical detail to add to this explanation of dimensions and measures. Tableau does not scan the values in your data items, which would be incredibly inefficient. Instead, it uses the metadata provided by your data source to identify and organize your dimensions and measures.

You can convert *measures* to *dimensions* and *dimensions* to *measures*, although more often you will convert *measures* to *dimensions* due to Tableau defaults. You can convert an item from *measure* to *dimension* **by dragging it from the Measures pane to the Dimensions pane, or you can right-click on it and select Convert to Dimension.** You can also perform this action on an item placed on a shelf if you need to convert the item for that particular view only.

For example, you may want to use *Discount* as a *dimension* so you can view all values separately rather than creating an axis from this field. In the following example, **the 1st scatter chart is the default Show Me! view for *Discount (Measure)*, *Gross Profit* and *Region* (with *Region* moved to the color shelf). The 2nd bar chart is the default Show Me! view for *Discount (Dimension)*, *Gross Profit* and *Region*.** Notice that the level of detail regarding *Discount* increases after it is converted to a *dimension*. As a measure, it displays one value for each region – the average discount for that region. As a dimension, all the unique values used in each region are shown.

Default Show Me! views: Discount (Measure) versus Discount (Dimension)

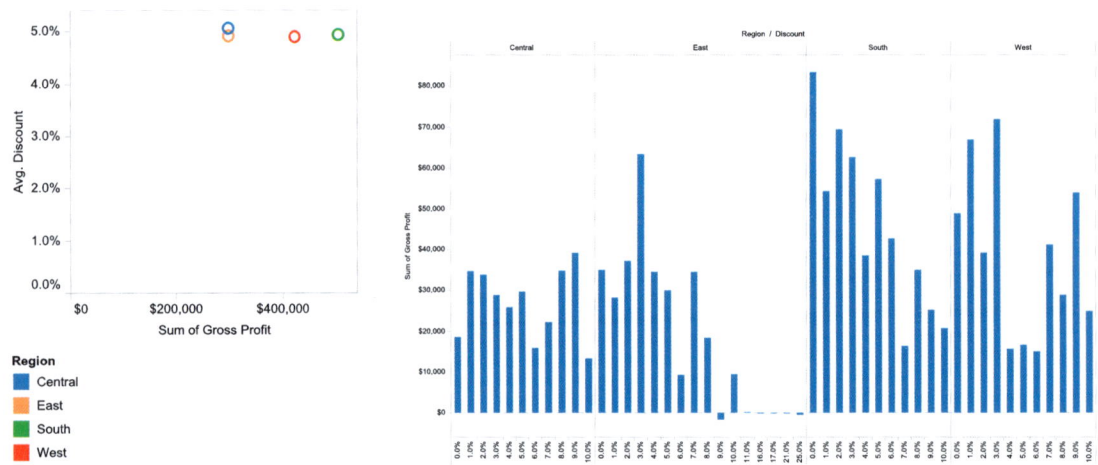

Continuous versus Discrete data items

In Tableau, all data items are classified as either **continuous** or **discrete**. In the Data Items pane, the icons located to the left of all data items are color-coded as green (*continuous*) or blue (*discrete*). When you add them to the Row or Column Shelves, *continuous* items always create axes and *discrete* items always create headers.

You can convert *continuous* items to *discrete* and *discrete* items to *continuous*, although more often you will convert *continuous* to *discrete* due to the Tableau defaults. **Do this by right-clicking on the item in the Data Items pane and selecting Convert to Discrete. If the change is required only for the current view, use the down carat next to the item to select Discrete.**

For example, you may want to change *Discount* to a *discrete* item. In this example, **the 1st continuous line chart is the default Show Me! view for *Discount (Continuous Dimension)* and *Gross Profit*. The 2nd bar chart is the default Show Me! view for *Discount (Discrete Dimension)* and *Gross Profit*.** Notice the very different representation of *Discount* as a *continuous* item versus a *discrete* item. The *continuous* graph has no gaps between the discount values, so it displays the long tail from 11% to 25% better than the *discrete* graph, which has separate marks for 11, 16, 17, 21 and 25%. Remember that both *measures* and *dimensions* can be converted from *continuous* to *discrete* items and vice-versa.

Default Show Me! views: Discount (Continuous) versus Discount (Discrete)

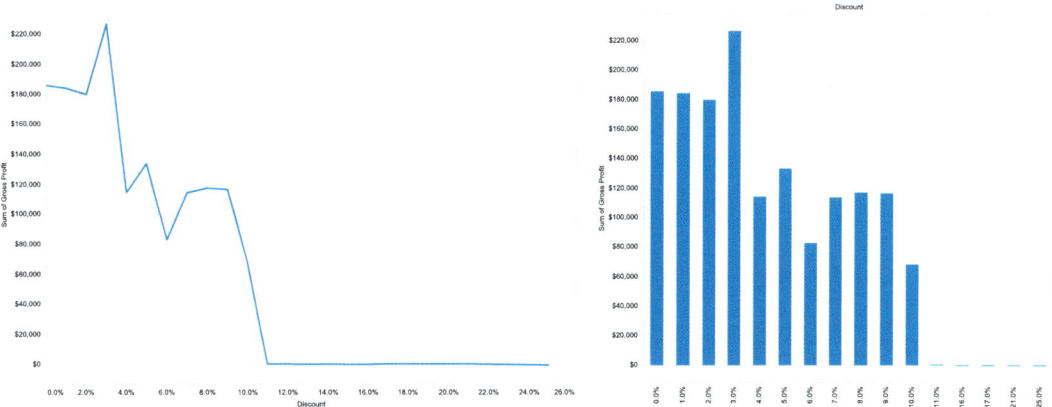

Default Mark Properties

All dimensional items have default mark properties that can be customized. You can customize them while they are still in the Data Items pane or after you add them to the view. The three mark properties are **Alias**, **Color** and **Shape**. *Alias* is how the text is displayed, for example changing "NE" to display as "Northeast". *Color* affects the default color for values, such as "Exceeds plan" displayed as green and "Below plan" displayed as red. *Shape* determines the default shape for a value, such as "Exceeds plan" could be 🟢 and "Below plan" could be 🔶. Note that only a few shapes have intrinsic color like these special KPI (Key Performance Indicators) shapes. Most shapes use the colors automatically specified for them by the Color shelf. Note that dates and continuous dimensions have no aliases since the actual values must be displayed.

To modify the mark properties from the Data Items pane, **right-click on the dimension item, select Edit Mark Properties and pick the mark type you wish to edit. Alternatively, you can place the item in the relevant view shelves and modify the properties from the shelf.** Changing mark properties of a data item from either the shelves or the view itself will modify the data item's overall mark properties, unless you have already changed the defaults from the Data Items pane itself. The next few figures are examples of what you can do if you adjust mark properties in various ways.

An "audience-friendly" alias for *Order Priority* - default versus customized

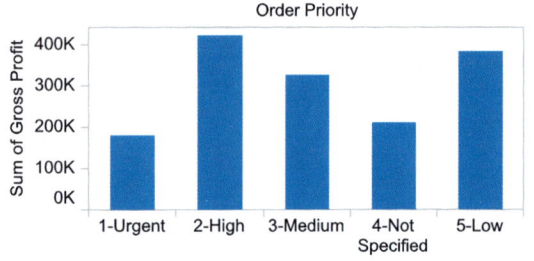

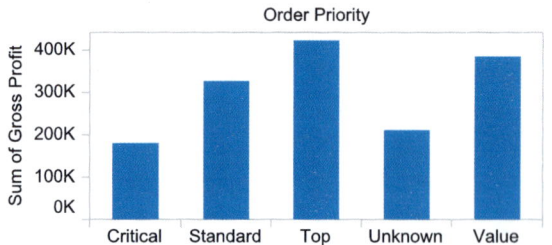

Color for *Order Priority* changed to be urgency-relevant: default versus customized (including manual sort of legend values)

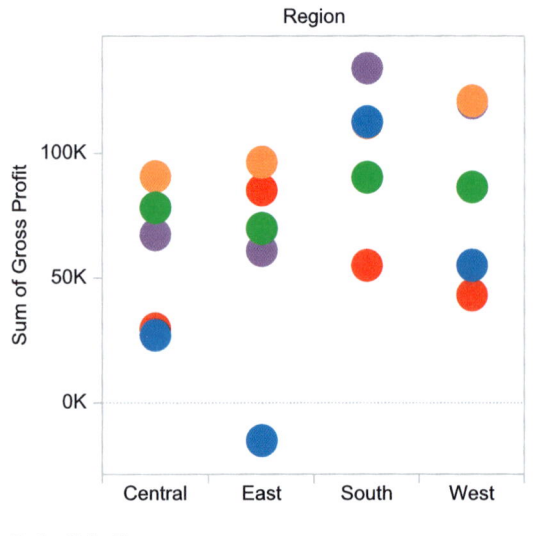

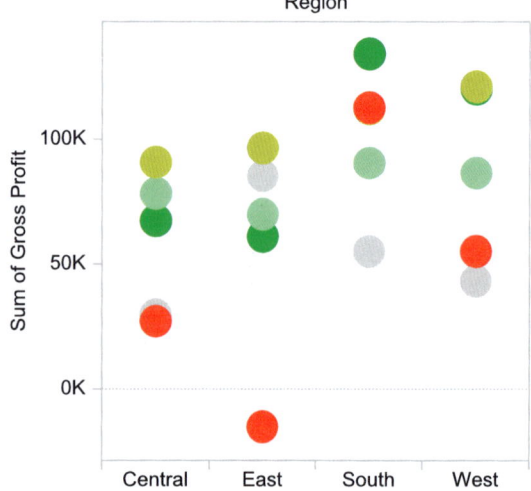

Order Priority

Order Priority

Shape for *Order Priority* changed to be "audience-friendly" based on corporate standards

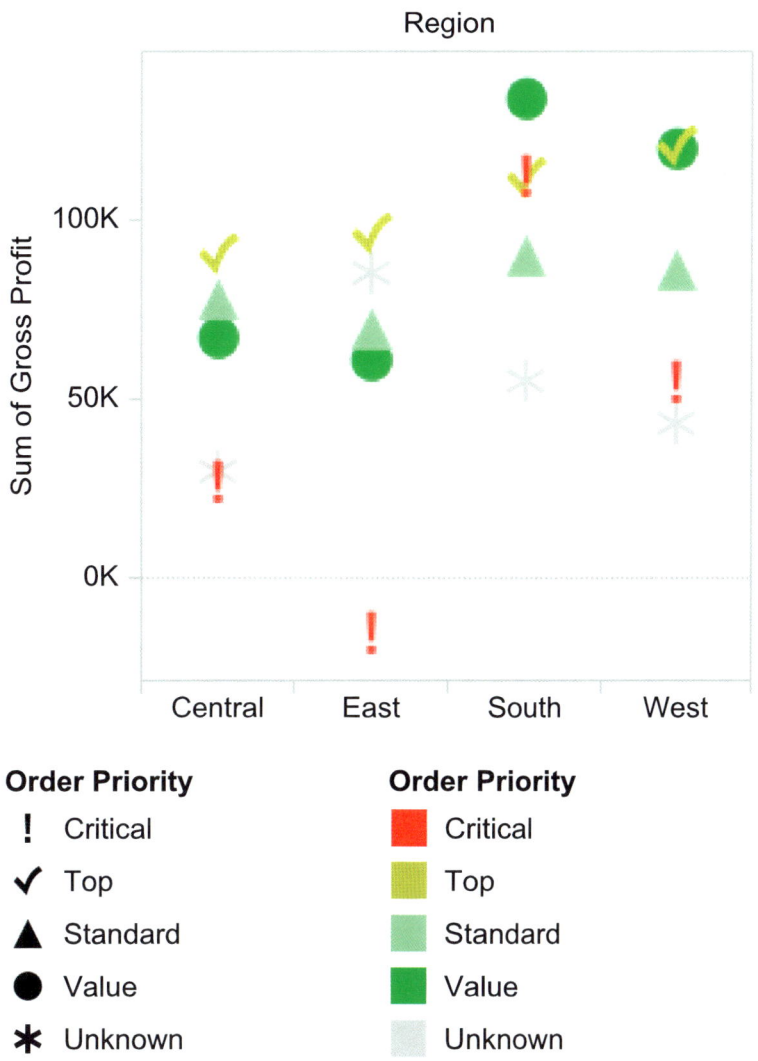

<u>*Default sorting, format and aggregation*</u>

All items have one or more selections available from the Set Default context menu. To pull this menu up, **right-click on an item, select Set Default, and then select the default option to change.** All dimensional items allow you to select a default sort order (e.g., order in original data source or by descending value). Date and number items allow you to specify a default date or number format (e.g., 0.08 or 8%, 1/1/2009 or January 1, 2009.) All measures except for geographic location items allow you to set a default aggregation (e.g., sum or average). Details about the aggregations available from this menu can be found in the Calculated Fields section in Chapter 9.

Note that sorting options from the Data Items pane are limited versus the Row or Columns shelves, but are the only way to control the sort on quick filters. Dimensional items on the shelf have an additional option of sorting by one of the dimension or measure items using a desired aggregation method. Several examples demonstrating advanced sorting, format and aggregation options follow.

Sort order example: *Ship Mode* sorted by default versus manually

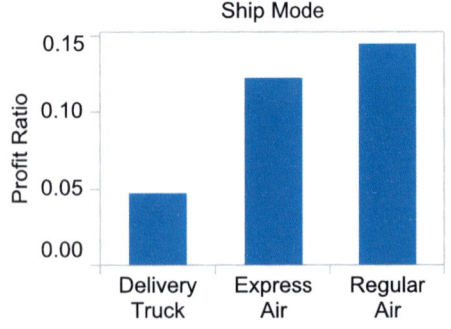
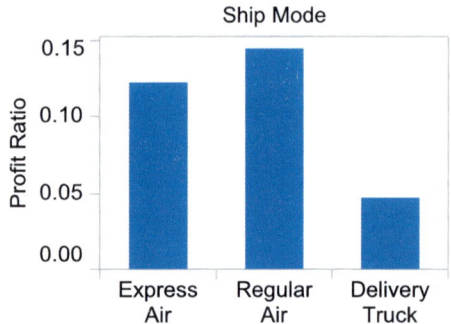

Number format example: default profit ratio format versus percent format

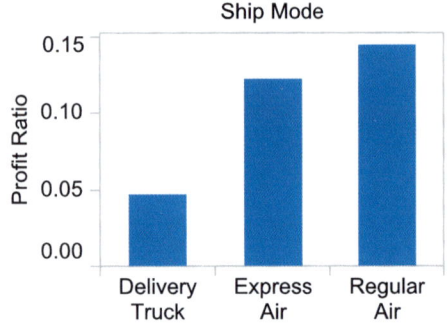
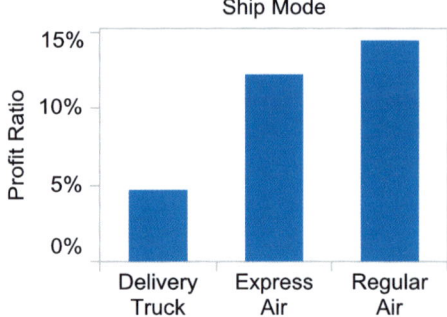

Aggregation example: default sum of *Gross Profit* versus *average Gross Profit*

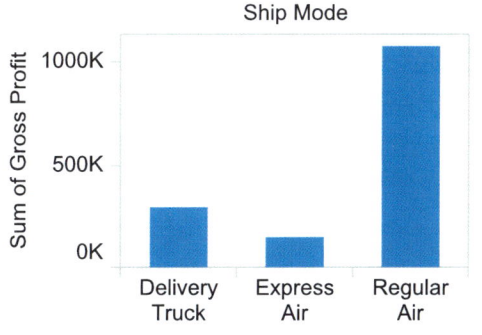 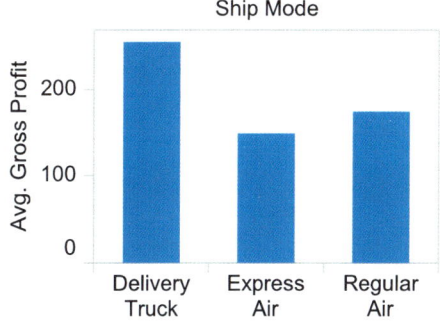

To create this last example, **turn off Aggregate Measures from the Analysis menu to display all records on view. Filter data for top 3 customers by Sum of Sales.** Note that all profit records for these top 3 customers are shown individually versus the aggregated bar chart views above.

No aggregation example: beyond default roles

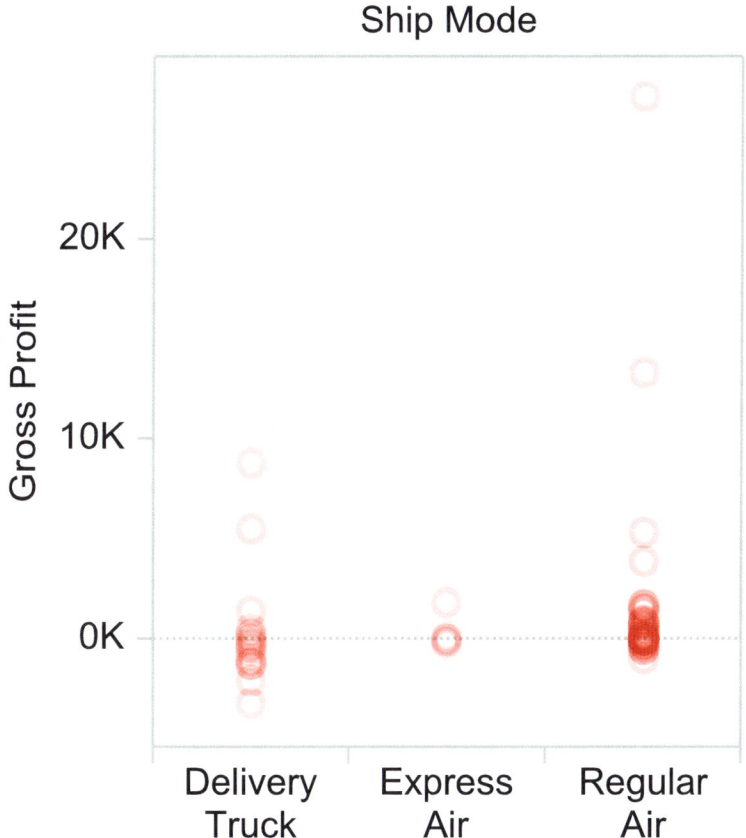

Geographic Roles put your data on the map

Tableau offers exciting mapping capabilities to overlay your data onto relevant maps. By default, data items that have certain names and data types within them are automatically assigned a geographic role. Items that could be one of the following are assigned a corresponding geographic role: Latitude and Longitude, Area Code (e.g., 206, 919), CMSA (U.S. Consolidated Metropolitan Statistical Area, e.g., Dallas-Fort Worth-Arlington), Country (FIPS 10 code), Country (ISO 3166-2, 2 character abbreviation), Country (ISO 3166-3, 3 character abbreviation), Country (Name in English), County (U.S. county names), State (Abbreviation, worldwide states and province abbreviations), State (Name, worldwide in English) and Zip Code (US 5 digit zip code). All other items have a default geographic role of None. Additionally, you can add your own geographic roles to extend the capabilities of Tableau, such as the location of your stores or all the airports in the world.

If Tableau does not properly identify your geographic item, you can change this role by **right-clicking on the item, selecting Geographic Role and choosing the proper geographic role from the above list.**

In case your dataset has some miscoded items that Tableau cannot map, **you can select Edit Locations from the Geographic Roles submenu to recode these items to their proper values.** See the following example demonstrating this with Zip Code data, which Tableau requires to be 5 digits in length. You can easily see that miscoded data will appear at 0 degrees longitude and 0 degrees latitude on your map!

Recoding unmatched location data in Tableau

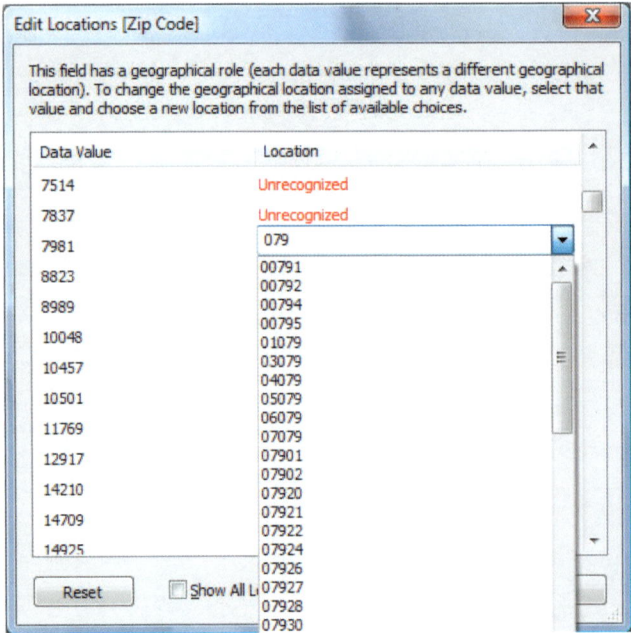

Zip code *Gross Profit* data without versus with mapping! Now you see it!

Other Useful Data Utilities- Replace References, Describe, Duplicate, Rename, Hide, Unhide, Hide All Unused Fields, Sort Data Items and Delete

Other simple data management utilities available from a data item's right-click menu include:

- **Replace References**: this very powerful command will replace all reference to the selected item in your Tableau Workbook with another item. *Be careful, this includes the use of the item in every sheet and in calculated items!* Of course, your views will reflect this change immediately.

- **Describe**: this command will give you very detailed information about the item including role, type, status (is it valid or not?), the formula used for the item and the domain of the item (this is a list of values or a range of values - **you must click Load** to see this, so do not do this for very large lists of distinct values!)

The Describe Field dialog- data item details

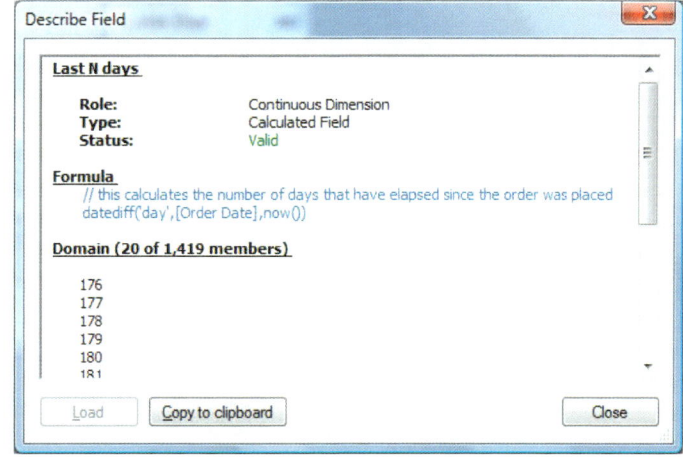

-

- **Duplicate**: this command will perform an equivalent of copy and paste all at once. You will see a duplicate version of the item copied with a new suffix on the item name, typically " (copy)" is appended to the original item name. Note that this does not modify your original data source; it merely creates a new item referencing it. This command is useful for reusing a calculate item formula or having the same item as a dimension and measure simultaneously.

- **Rename:** this command allows you to rename an item with a name more relevant for your workbook.

- **Hide**: irrelevant or potentially confusing items can be hidden from users of your workbook with this command. No changes are made to your original data source when you use this command; the item simply is not displayed in your Data Items pane. Hiding also removes the item from view underlying data and prevents it from being extracted.

- **Unhide:** when you hide one or more items, a special information icon ⓘ appears at the upper right part of the Dimensions or Measures pane. When you hover over this icon, you will see how many items are hidden from view for the Dimensions or Measures pane. To unhide items, **click on the dropdown menu beside the icon and select "Show Hidden Fields".** The hidden fields will appear in the pane as grayed out items. **You must right-click on the item and select unhide for it to be available for use in your workbook.**

- **Hide All Unused Fields**: this command will hide all fields not currently in use in the workbook. This is very useful for simplifying the Data Items pane list from large data sources. To hide all unused items, **click on the dropdown menu at the upper right of the Dimensions or Measures pane and select "Hide All Unused Fields".**

- **Sort Data Items**: the data items in the Dimensions and Measures panes are sorted by their names by default. If you would prefer to see them ordered by their original data source order, **click on the dropdown menu at the upper right of the Dimensions or Measures pane and select Sort By -> Data Source Order**. This is very useful for very wide tables that have the items in a particular order.

- **Delete:** this command is only available for calculated fields. All other fields can be hidden. The main difference is that once a calculated item is deleted, there is no way to recover it in the current workbook once your session is closed (until then, it can be recovered using Undo functionality).

View Underlying Data- understand the detail behind the View

This powerful feature allows you to see a table of all records used in your view. If you select specific data points in your view **(using <Ctrl> and click or clicking and dragging over parts of the view to select them),** the view underlying data feature will only show you the rows behind the selected data items. This is particularly useful for examining unusual data values in your view for additional detail. **Simply right-click on your view and select View Underlying Data**.

Highlighting a data point in a view and viewing underlying data

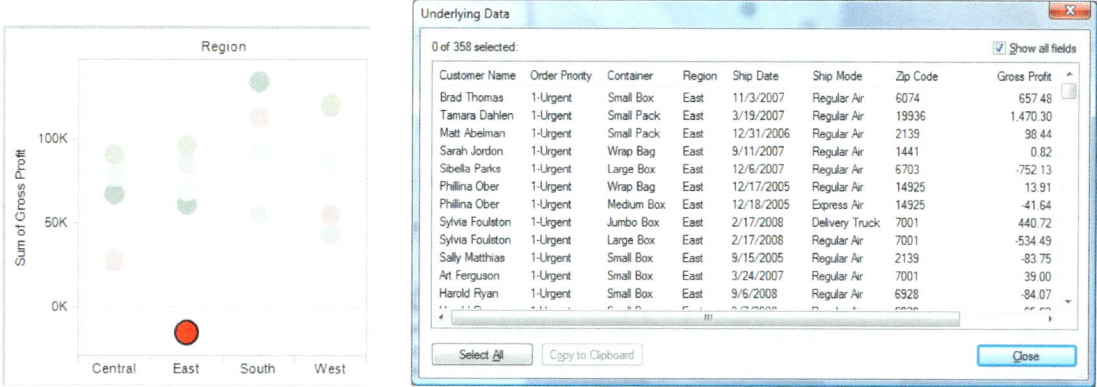

From the Underlying Data dialog, you have quite a few viewing options. **You can resize any field by dragging the side of the header, you can sort by a field by clicking on the header and you can turn off all other fields not used in the current view by clicking on Show all fields**.

As you review the data, **you can select rows with click and the <Shift> key, which allows selection of a range of rows, or the <Ctrl> key, which allows selection of multiple specific rows.** If desired, **you can select all rows by clicking on the Select All button.** Once you have selected the desired rows, you can copy them to your Windows clipboard **by clicking on Copy to Clipboard.** You can paste the results into Excel, Word and many other applications, including Tableau!

Dividing numeric data items into intervals using Bins

A data bin enables you to divide a numeric data item into equally sized intervals or "bins". For example, suppose you would like to organize sales transactions into 20 intervals based on sales amount. If you requested to bin sales amount (sales amounts ranging from $0 to $1,000) into 20 bins, Tableau would create bins each having a sales amount length of $50 (e.g., $0-$50, $50-$100, $100-$150, and so on up to $950-$1,000). To do this, you would **right-click on *Sales* and select Create Bins**. The Create Bins dialog appears. Unless your data source is very large, you would typically **click on Load** to see the range of values in this field.

The Create Bins dialog for *Sales* (select Load to see the range of values)

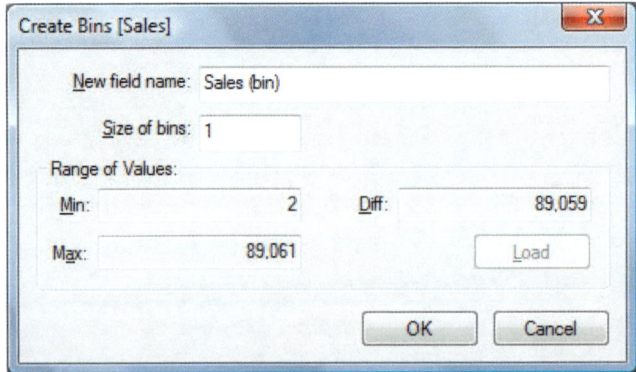

To create 20 similar sized intervals, **simply divide the difference between the maximum and minimum values (called Diff in this dialog) by 20- in this example, you would use 4,500 after rounding up.**

! *Alternate Route:* If you display your data item in a histogram, Tableau automatically bins the item for you.

Bins are very useful for understanding the number of records occurring within each bin (or value range) or examining the total or average value within ranges, as shown in the following examples. In both charts, you can see most transactions are in the first bin and almost every transaction is in the first six bins. The first chart displays *Count of Sales*, with virtually every sale in the first bin. Examining the second chart depicting *Sum of Sales*, you can see a very different story.   While the first bin is still the largest, it is only around 1/3 of the total *Sum of Sales*. Therefore, the relatively small number of transactions in the remaining bins yield around 2/3 of all sales dollars.

Sales binned and displayed in two views: *Count of Sales* versus *Sum of Sales*

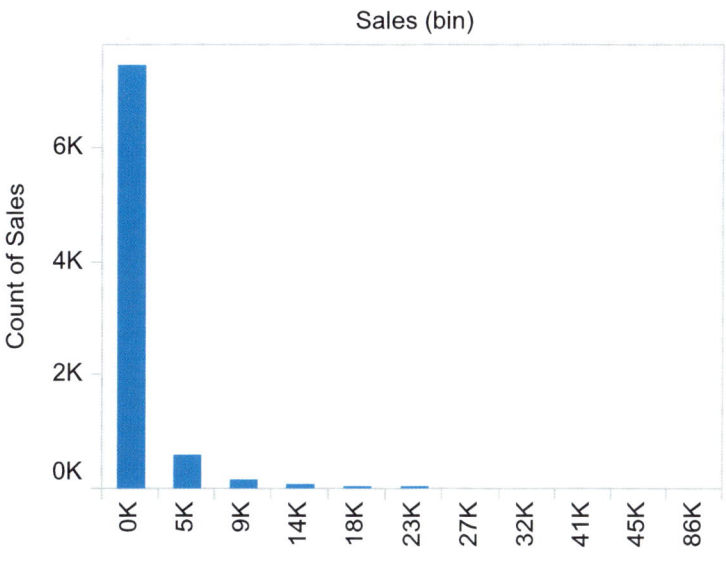

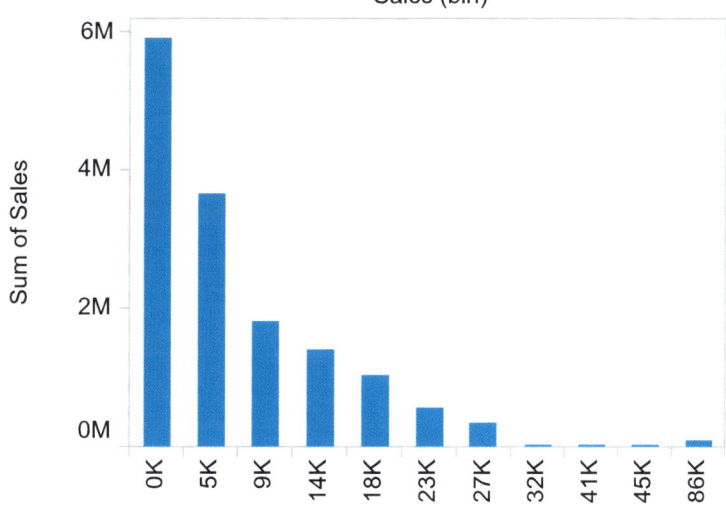

Grouping dimensions into categories

Tableau allows rapid grouping of selected values from a dimensional item. For example, suppose you want to create group product categories into three groups of roughly equal sales to assign responsibility among three new product managers. In the example below, you can see the product categories before and after grouping.

Grouping *Product Categories* into three similar sized groups to distribute sales volume among Product Managers

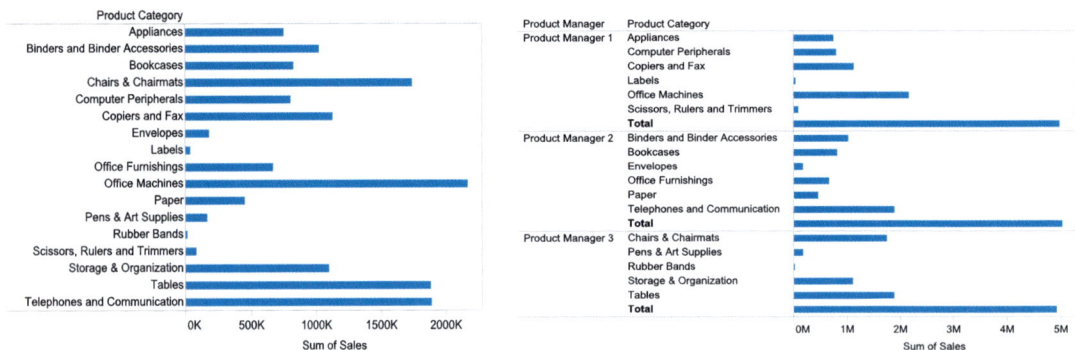

Grouping values directly from the view allows you to leverage the information from other relevant data items. From the view, **you can <Ctrl> and click or <Shift> and click to select multiple values, then right-click to select the Group command.** After you have completed grouping values, **you can rename the grouped values by right-clicking on the grouped values and selecting Edit Alias.** The Edit Alias dialog appears, as shown below. **Then click on the values and rename the grouped values.**

Renaming values after grouping from the view

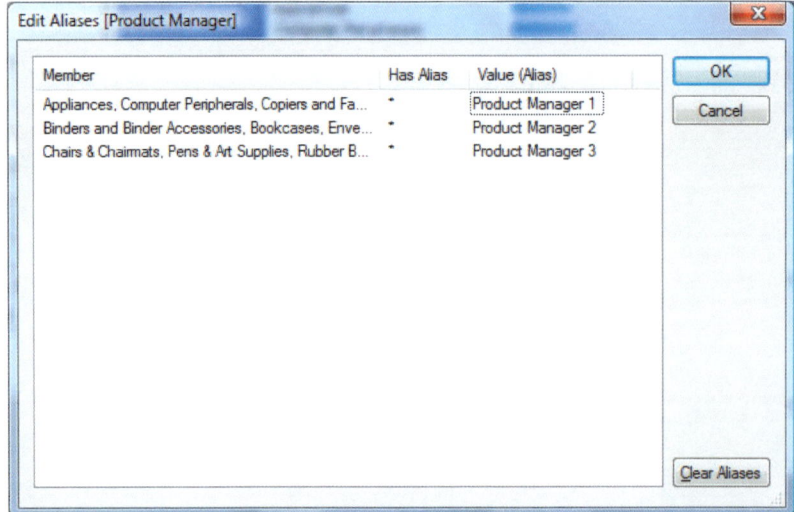

Note that grouping values from the view automatically creates a new dimension item with the same name as the grouped item, with "(group)" added to the name. Additional grouping functionality is available by **right-clicking on the newly created dimension item from the Data Items pane and selecting Edit** so that the Edit Group dialog appears (shown below).

The Edit Group dialog: Group, Ungroup, Rename, and Group "Other" values

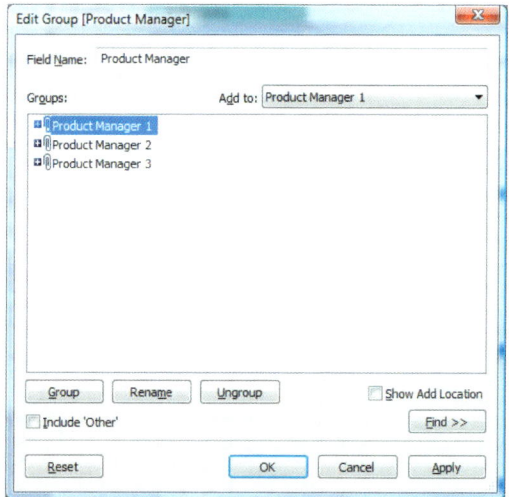

All view-based grouping functionality is available from this dialog, along with some additional features. The view-based grouping approach assumes all values of the data item are available. However, if a new value appears in the data after defining the group, it will be ignored unless you specify where to include the "Other" values, a catchall for values not explicitly categorized. You can ungroup values by **clicking on the group and selecting Ungroup. Then drag ungrouped values to an existing group or create a new group by selecting them and clicking Group.** Another powerful feature from this dialog is the ability to find values within the groups by **clicking on Find**, which expands the Edit Group dialog to add a Find sub-dialog area, shown below with all values containing "office" highlighted.

The Find functionality within the Edit Group dialog

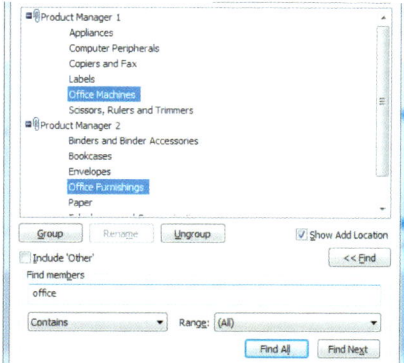

The power of Sets to combine and filter your View

Sets are custom fields that are similar to groups but more powerful because they can be created from one or more existing dimension items. All sets can function as advanced, pre-defined filters or placed on the Rows or Columns shelves as data items. You can have a simple set based on a single dimension item, such as including all order quantities of more than 5 items. A set based on two or more items behaves as a complex item combining all the unique combinations of the selected dimension item levels in your set. For example, a set could contain all sales amounts greater than $80 with a gross profit greater than $40, or all female customers who shopped at our store before 1999.

Three frequent applications of sets include:

- Create a subset of one or more dimension items that can be reused in other worksheets as an item with an automated filter based on the levels selected. For example, **click on** *Sales* **and** *Gross Profit* **and select Show Me!, accepting the default Scatter view type. Add** *Order Priority* **to the Color shelf and** *Region* **to the Shape shelf**. A chart similar to the following figure appears. **Highlight some of the points in the upper right quadrant by <Ctrl> and clicking on them. Right-click over the selected items and select Create Set** and the Create Set From Selection dialog appears. **Name the set "High Total Sales and Profit" and click OK**. The new set will appear in the bottom of the Data Items pane with this special set icon, 🔴, next to the item.

Create a set from a scatter plot

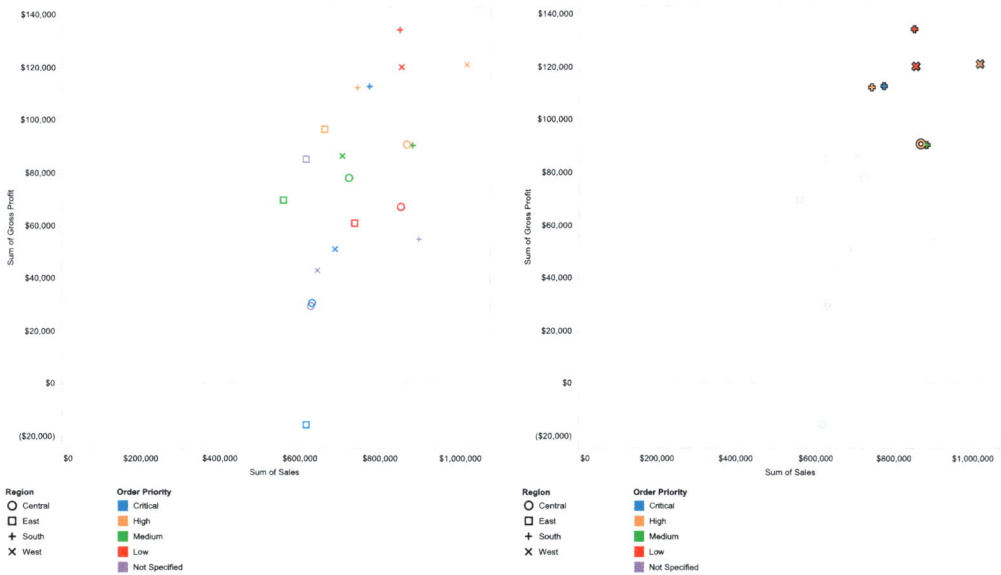

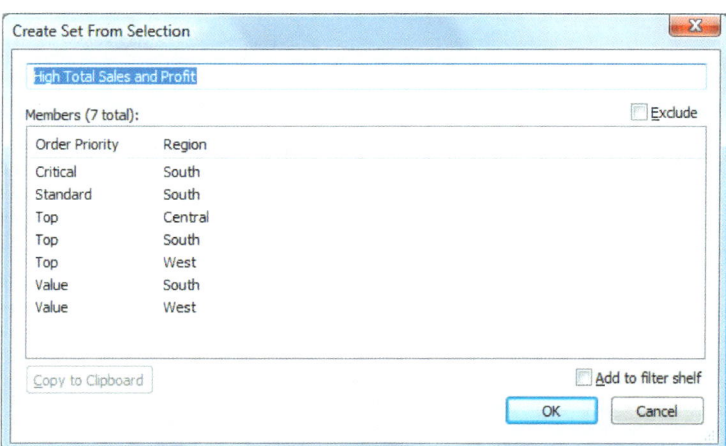

- Create a unique combination of two or more dimension items to create a new set. For example, create a set that combines *Region* and *Order Priority* into a new item. **Clicking on *Region*, hold down the <Ctrl> key, click on *Order Priority*, and then right-click and select Create Set**. The Create Set dialog appears- **name the set "Order Priority and Region", click OK**.

- Save an existing filter as a set for later use. Using any of the filter functionality, you can reuse the filter in your workbook repeatedly as a set, a great time saver! Conceptually, this is very similar to highlighting values from a scatter plot and creating a set. To use this capability, **right-click on a filter in your workbook and select Create Set**.

You can use a set just like any other dimension item. You can add a set to a shelf or to filters. However, no matter where you add a set to your view, it is always added as a filter.

! *Performance Tip:* Note that if you use a filter and a set based on the same dimension, the result will be what the filter and the set have in common (also called the intersection of the two).

From the set creation examples in this section, **add the *Order Priority* and *Region* set to the rows shelf and *Gross Profit* to the columns shelf**, this creates a bar chart similar to the following example. Note that the values are a combination of *Order Priority* and *Region* separated by a comma; this is a set functioning as a combination of items. **Now, add the High Total Sales and Profit set to the Filters**. This updates the bar chart to show only the data for the values selected in the earlier scatter plot.

Sets as a combination of multiple items and a reusable filter

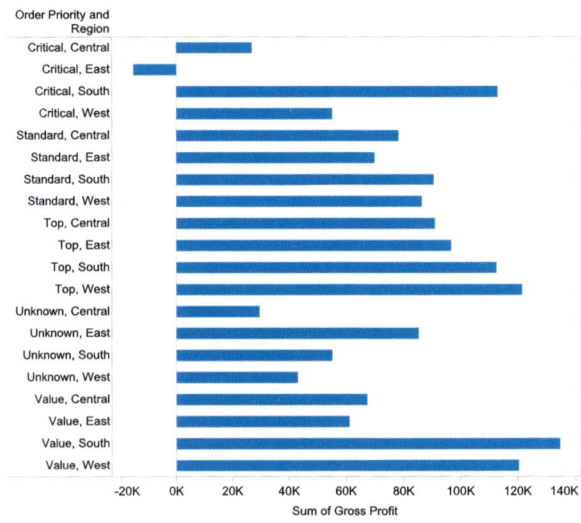

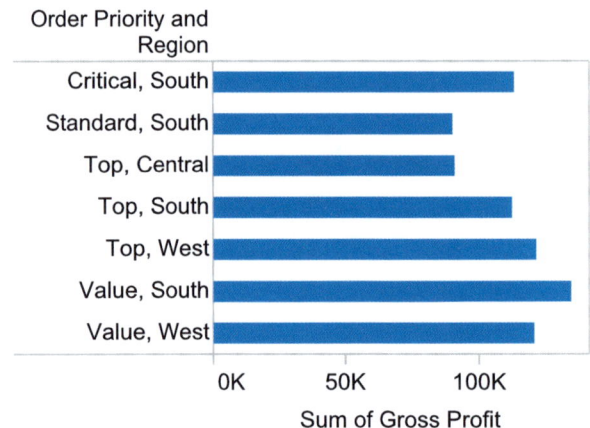

Chapter 9

Advanced data management in Tableau

Chapter Highlights

- Calculated Fields- the power to shape your data

- Functions- keys to powerful calculated fields grouped by data type usage

    o   Numeric

    o   Character

    o   Date

    o   Logical

    o   Type Conversion

    o   Aggregate

- Queries- from simple to multi-table data queries

- Extracts- accelerate your analysis and work away from the office

---

In Chapter 8, you learned the secrets to great data management using Tableau. This chapter will build upon that knowledge by covering advanced topics such as calculated fields and the many functions available in Tableau to create exactly the data items you need for an analysis. The chapter concludes with an overview of queries and Tableau data extracts.

Examples in this chapter use the sample data source that you worked with in Chapter 8- the **Sample – Superstore Sales (Excel)**.

Calculated Fields- power to answer your difficult questions

Sometimes you may need a field that your original data source does not include, but that you could calculate using the current fields. For example, you might want to create a new calculated field called Profit Ratio, the ratio of the profit field to the sales field. Another example would be to create a conditional statement called "Shipping Commitment Met" that determines if the actual time to ship was greater than the promised time to ship, returning a value of 1 if true or 0 if false.

To create a new calculated field, **right-click on a field you want to include in the calculation and select Create Calculated Field**. The Calculated Field dialog will appear as shown below.

The Calculated Field dialog

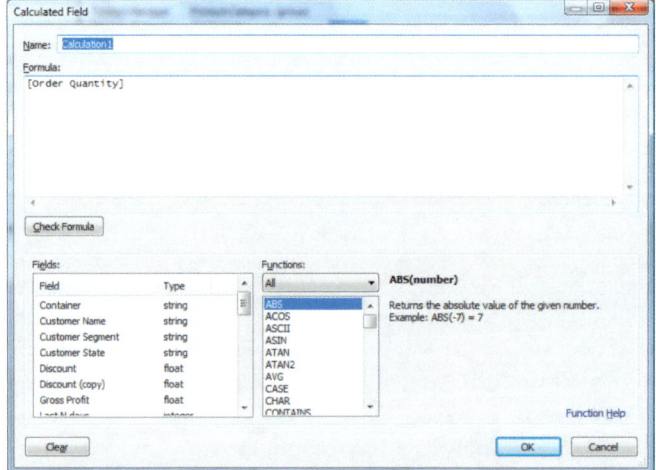

From the Calculated Field dialog, you can name the new calculated field, enter the formula for the new field, check the entered formula to see if it is valid, add fields from the Fields pane, find functions by category and add them to the formula and see the definition of the function in the lower right hand space above the OK button. Using fields and functions, you can create simple to very complex calculations to fit a wide array of situations.

This section contains a detailed list of the Calculated Field Operators and a set of tables that organizes the groupings available in the Functions dropdown from the Calculated Field dialog. Each function includes syntax details and examples using the function. It is important to note that some functions modify a field (e.g., the left function takes part of the original field and returns it) while other functions test a field or compare fields and return a status back to the calculation (e.g., the length function returns the length of a field while the IF, THEN, ELSE functions check for conditions and returns a value specified by you if true and another value specified by you if false.)

Calculated Field Operators

To create calculated fields, it is crucial to understand the field operators available in Tableau. The basic operators are shown here in the order of precedence that operator calculations will occur (i.e., addition is calculated by Tableau before any multiplication occurs.)

Operator	Details
+	• Addition when used with numbers. • Combining or concatenation when used with strings. • When used with date fields, it will add the specified number of days to a date: ○ *#June 1, 2009# + 1* will return *#June 2, 2009#* ○ " #" marks surround a date value in Tableau (more on this later)
-	• Subtraction when used with numbers: ○ "78-10" will return "68". ○ [Sales]-[Expenses] will return the gross profit from each transaction from a relational data source. • Negation if applied to an expression. • When used with dates, subtracts the specified number of days from a date. • Calculate the difference in days between two dates.
*	• Used for numeric multiplication: 12*7 will return 84.
/	• Used for numeric division: 12/6 will return 2.

Comparison operators that can be used in expressions:

Operator	Definition	Example
= = or =	equal to	1=2 is false
>	greater than	1>2 is false
<	less than	1<2 is true
>=	greater than or equal to	1.1>=(1+0.1) is true
<=	less than or equal to	1.1<=1.2 is false
!= or <>	not equal to	1.1!=1.1 is false

All operators can compare two numbers, dates, or strings. They all return a Boolean value, TRUE or FALSE. Note that Boolean values cannot be compared using these operators. For example, FALSE=FALSE is not a valid expression. To compare Booleans with operators, use the logical operators AND or OR. For example, TRUE AND TRUE is a valid expression returning TRUE.

In the following tables:

- [Number] refers to any number you type (e.g., 7.8 or -14/3).
- [Item] refers to a valid item from your data source.
- [String] refers to a string you type in (e.g., "Tableau" or "Beauty").
- Singular refers to functions that return the same number of rows as your data source.
- Aggregate categories collapse your data to a smaller number of rows based on your view layout.

Category	Function	Syntax	Example
Numeric (Singular)	**Round a number** to a specified number of digits.	ROUND([Number],decimal) or ROUND([Item],decimal or [Decimal Item]) decimal is optional, [Number] of decimal places	ROUND(10.47)=10 ROUND(10.47,1)=10.5 ROUND([Height],1)= height rounded for each row in the table
Numeric (Singular)	**Absolute value** of a number or absolute value of each value in a database item.	ABS([Number]) or ABS([Item])	ABS(-10.1)=10.1 ABS(18.2)=18.2 ABS([Profit])=all rows in item as non-negative numbers
Numeric (Singular)	**Sign of a number**- negative, positive or zero. Negative is returned as -1, positive as 1, and zero as 0.	SIGN([Number]) or SIGN([Item])	SIGN(-3.5)=-1 SIGN([Sales])= sign for each row in the table
Numeric (Singular)	**Square of a number.**	SQUARE([Number]) or SQUARE([item])	SQUARE(6)=36 SQUARE([item])=square for each row in the table
Numeric (Singular)	**Raise a number to a power.**	POWER([Number],power) or Power([Item],power or [Power Item])	POWER(10,3) = 1000 POWER([LogWeight],2)= weight to the second power for each row in the table
Numeric (Singular)	**Square root of a number.** Returns Null for values of zero or less.	SQRT([Number]) or SQRT([item])	SQRT(36)=6 SQRT([item])=square root for each row in the table
Numeric (Singular)	**Logarithm of a number for a given base.** Returns the exponent needed to raise the base to that number.	LOG([Number],base) or LOG([Item],base or [Base Item]) base is optional, defaults to	LOG(1000) = 3 LOG([Weight])= logarithm base 10 for each row in the table
Numeric (Singular)	**Natural logarithm of a number.** Returns the exponent needed to raise *e* to that number, or Null if number is zero or less.	LN([Number]) or LN([Item])	LN(7.389) = 2 LN([Weight])=natural logarithm for each row in the table
Numeric (Singular)	**e or Euler's number raised to a power.** *e* is approximately 2.7128 and is commonly used in exponential functions.	EXP([Number]) or EXP([Item])	EXP(2) = 7.389 EXP(-[Growth Rate]*[Time])=e to the power of the negative two items multiplied for each row in the table

130

Category	Function	Syntax	Example
Character (Modify Values in String)	**Remove all left or right trailing spaces only** (two similar functions).	LTRIM([String]) or RTRIM([String]) or LTRIM([Item]) or RTRIM([Item])	LTRIM(" Cool ")="Cool " or RTRIM(" Cool ")=" Cool" or LTRIM([Item]) or RTRIM([Item])
Character (Modify Values in String)	**Remove all leading and trailing spaces in string.**	TRIM([String]) or TRIM([Item])	TRIM(" Cool data ")="Cool data" or TRIM([Name])
Character (Modify Values in String)	**Upper case** the characters of a string.	UPPER([String]) or UPPER([Item])	UPPER("Stephen 7") = "STEPHEN 7" or UPPER([Name])= names upper cased for each row in the table
Character (Modify Values in String)	**Lower case** the characters of a string.	LOWER([String]) or LOWER([Item])	LOWER("Stephen 7") = "stephen 7" or LOWER([Name])= names lower cased for each row in the table
Character (Modify Values in String)	**Return the 1ˢᵗ n characters** of a string (leftmost characters).	LEFT([String],[Number]) or LEFT([Item],[Number] or [Length Item])	LEFT("Stephen 7",3)="Ste" or LEFT([Name],3)= 1ˢᵗ 3 characters for each row in the table
Character (Modify Values in String)	**Return the middle n characters** of a string starting at a certain character location.	MID([String],start, *length*) or LEFT([Item], start, *length*) Items can be start and length, length optional	MID("Stephen 7",4)="phen 7" or MID("Stephen 7",4,2)="ph" or MID([Name],3)
Character (Modify Values in String)	**Return the rightmost characters** of a string.	LEFT([String],[Number]) or LEFT([Item],[Number] or [Length Item])	RIGHT("Stephen 7 ",3)=" 7 " or RIGHT([Name],3)= Last 3 characters for each row in the table

Category	Function	Syntax	Example
Character (Locate Values in String)	**Test whether a specified string is within a string. Returns True or False value. This is case sensitive!**	CONTAINS([String], specified string) or CONTAINS([Name], specified string) or CONTAINS([Name], [Specified String Item])	CONTAINS("Stephen","J")= False or CONTAINS("Stephen","eph")= True or CONTAINS([Name], [Specified String Item])
Character (Locate Values in String)	**Find the position of the 1st instance of a specified string in a string.** Returns 0 if not found. Can specify starting find character location.	FIND([String], substring, *start*), start is optional, or FIND([Item], substring, *start*)	FIND(" Stephen ","eph")=4 or FIND(" Stephen ","eph",5) =0 or FIND([Name],"eph")=location of 'eph' in each row of a table
Character (Locate Values in String)	**Length of a string.** Includes leading and trailing spaces.	LEN([String]) or LEN([Item])	LEN(" Stephen ")=9 or LEN([Name])= length of each row in a table
Character (Locate Values in String)	**Test whether a specified string is at the start of a string.** Returns True or False value. This is case sensitive! Ignores leading spaces.	STARTSWITH([String], specified string) or STARTSWITH([Name], specified string)	STARTSWITH("Stephen ","Jo") = False or STARTSWITH ("Stephen ","St") = True
Character (Locate Values in String)	**Test whether a specified string is at the end of a string.** Returns True or False value. This is case sensitive! Ignores trailing spaces.	ENDSWITH([String], specified string) or ENDSWITH([Name], specified string) or ENDSWITH([Name], [Specified String Item])	ENDSWITH("Stephen ","J")= False or ENDSWITH ("Stephen ","en")= True or ENDSWITH([Name], [Specified String Item])

Date Functions

The following examples use the **#** symbol to surround date expressions. This instructs Tableau to interpret the information between the # symbols as a "Date Literal" and convert it to an internal date value (number) that can be used with addition and subtraction operations.   Some of these functions use date_part, which is constant string argument. The valid date_part values that you can use are 'year' (four digit year), 'quarter' (1-4), 'month' (1-12 or "January", "February", etc.), 'dayofyear' Day of the year (Jan 1 is 1, Feb 1 is 32, etc.), 'day' (1-31), 'weekday' (1-7 or "Sunday", "Monday", etc.), 'week' (1-53), 'hour" (0-23), 'minute' (0-59) and 'second' (0-60).

Category	Function	Syntax	Example
Date (Create Item)	**Return the current date or date and time.** Two similar functions.	TODAY() or NOW()	TODAY()=#June 16, 2009# or NOW()=#June 16, 2009 8:10:06 PM#
Date (Item Calculation)	**Calculate the difference between two dates expressed in specified increments.** For example, find the number of months between two dates.	DATEDIFF([Date Unit], [Base Date], [Compare Date])	DATEDIFF('month', #July 30, 2004#, #August 1, 2004#) = 1 or DATEDIFF('month', #July 1, 2004#, #August 30, 2004#) = 1

Category	Function	Syntax	Example
Date (Modify Item)	**Add or subtract a specified amount of date increment(s) to a date.** For example, add 3 months or 3 years to the date.	DATEADD([Date Unit], increment amount, [Date]) [Date Unit] = "day", "week" ,"month", "quarter" or "year"	DATEADD('month',2, #December 15, 2004#) = #January 15, 2005#
Date (Modify Item)	**Return just part of the date as a string.** For example, return the month or the year of a date.	DATENAME([Date Unit], [Date]) [Date Unit] = "day", "week" ,"month", "quarter" or "year"	DATENAME('month', #May 15, 2004#) = "May" or DATENAME('year', #May 15, 2004#) = "2004"
Date (Modify Item)	**Return just part of the date as an integer.** For example, return the month or the year of a date as a number.	DATEPART([Date Unit], [Date]) [Date Unit] = "day", "week" ,"month", "quarter" or "year"	DATENAME('month', #May 15, 2004#) = 5 or DATENAME('year', #May 15, 2004#) = 2004
Date (Modify Item)	**Truncate the date to the start of the unit specified.** For example, truncate a date to the 1st day of a quarter.	DATETRUNC([Date Unit], [Date]) [Date Unit] = "day", "week" ,"month", "quarter" or "year"	DATETRUNC('month', #May 15, 2004#) = #May 1, 2004# or DATETRUNC('year', #May 15, 2004#) = #January 1, 2004#
Date (Modify Item)	**Return the day, month, or year of the date as an integer.** These are three similar functions.	DAY([Date]) MONTH([Date]) YEAR([Date])	DAY(#May 15, 2004#) = 15 MONTH(#May 15, 2004#) = 5 YEAR(#May 15, 2004#) = 2004

Type Conversion

You can covert the result of any calculation to a specific data type. The conversion functions are DATE, DATETIME, INT, STR and FLOAT. For example, if you want to convert a floating-point number like 12.8 as an integer, INT(12.8) would return 13. Note that a Boolean can be converted to an integer, floating number or a string.

Category	Function	Syntax	Example
Data Type Conversion	Convert a number or string to a date.	DATE([Number] or string)	DATE("June 18, 2009") = #June 18, 2009# or DATE(#2009-06-18 18:06#)
Data Type Conversion	Convert a number or string to a date time.	DATETIME([Number] or string)	DATE(#2009-06-18 18:06#) = #2009-06-18 18:06:00#
Data Type Conversion	Convert a number or string to an integer. Before converting to an integer, the value is rounded.	INT([Number] or string)	INT(1)=1 or INT(-1/3)=0 or INT(1.5)=1 or INT(1.50001)=2
Data Type Conversion	Convert a date or a number to a string.	STR([Date] or [Number])	STR(#June 18, 2009#) = "June 18, 2009" or STR(1.05)="1.05"
Data Type Conversion	Convert a string, integer, or date to a floating-point number. A floating-point number could be 3.000 or 3.1415.	FLOAT([String] or [Number] or [Date]) Note that there must be no commas or other symbols in the value.	FLOAT(#June 18, 2009#) = 39,982.000 or FLOAT("1.05")=1.05

Category	Function	Syntax	Example
Logical	**Simple logical test to check whether something is true or false and return a specified value.**	IIF(logical test, true value, false value, [unknown value]) [unknown value] is a catch all if the logical test can't be evaluated, generally due to a NULL in the logical test. Note that it is generally a good idea to use the [unknown value] catchall.	IIF([Profit]>[Budget Profit], "Cool", "Lame", "Huh?") For [Profit]=100, [Budget Profit]=102 Value returned="Lame" or IIF([Items]!=0, [Sales]/[Items], 0, NULL) For [Items]=10, [Sales]=45 Value returned=4.5
Logical	**Extended logical test to check whether something is true or false repeatedly and return a specified value.**	IF logical test THEN true value ELSEIF logical test THEN true value ELSEIF *repeat many logical tests* THEN repeat *true value* ELSE unknown value END	IF [Sales] >= [Sales Plan]*1.2 THEN "Awesome" ELSEIF [Sales] < [Sales Plan]*0.8 THEN "Disappointing" ELSEIF [Sales] >= [Sales Plan]*1 THEN "Strong" ELSEIF [Sales] < [Sales Plan]*1 THEN "Just Below" ELSE "Unknown" END For [Sales]=90, [Sales Plan]=100 Value returned="Just Below"
Logical	**Simple expression checked repeatedly against values to check whether there is a match and return a specified value.**	CASE expression WHEN value THEN true value WHEN next value THEN next true value [ELSE catch all value] END [ELSE catch all value] is used if none of the values match the expression used	CASE LOWER(LEFT([Company],3)) WHEN "tab" THEN "Tableau" WHEN "fre" THEN "Freakalytics" ELSE "Another company" END For [Company]="fREakolytcs" Value returned="Freakalytics"

Category	Function	Syntax	Example
Multiple-Date, Numeric, String (Aggregate)	**Minimum** of two values or minimum of all values in a database item, null values are ignored	MIN(date , [Date]) MIN([Number] , [Number]) MIN([String] , string) or	MIN(1,2)=1 MIN(Stephen, Eileen)=Eileen MIN([Sales]) = smallest sales amount in table
Multiple-Date, Numeric, String (Aggregate)	**Maximum** of two values or maximum of all values in a database item, null values are ignored	MAX(date , [Date]), MAX([Number], [Number]), MAX([String] , string), or MAX([Item])	MAX(1,2)=2 MAX(Stephen, Eileen)=Stephen MAX([Sales]) = largest value in table
Any Data Type (Aggregate)	**Count the number of rows** in a database item, excludes null rows from count.	COUNT([Item]) Unavailable with Excel, Access, and text files. Create a Tableau extract from to use with these data sources.	COUNT([Sales]) = number of sales rows in table that are not null.
Any Data Type (Aggregate)	**Count the number of distinct rows** in a database item, excludes null rows from distinct count.	COUNTD([Item]) Unavailable with Excel, Access, and text files. Create a Tableau extract from to use with these data sources.	COUNTD([Sales]) = number of unique sales values in table that are not null (if there are 10 sales values but ½ are $5 and the other half are $10, the returned value would be 2.
Numeric (Aggregate)	**SUM** of all values in a database item, null values are ignored.	SUM([Item])	SUM([Sales]) = sum of all values in table, null values are ignored.
Numeric (Aggregate)	**AVG** of all values in a database item, null values are ignored.	AVG([Item])	AVG([Sales]) = average of all values in table, null values are ignored.

Queries to retrieve the data you need

By default, Tableau automatically connects you with single tables in your data source. Some data sources may contain only one table, while other sources have many tables to select from and use as data sources. It is beyond the scope of this book to explain how to connect and optimize the multiple data sources that Tableau can connect with- please see the online help from Tableau for extensive coverage of this topic (**Help -> Help Topics**).

Additionally, Tableau allows you to join two or more tables from your data source via a dialog or using custom SQL (query commands written by you!). Explaining how to write custom SQL is beyond the scope of this book. However, there are many excellent books to learn SQL programming and some that are specific to SQL specifically for popular databases. Although this book does not cover the details of writing SQL, please note that you can see the SQL Tableau has written for you based on the options you have selected from **Data -> Data Connection -> Edit**. Learning Custom SQL can be very helpful when working with extremely large data sources (more than tens of millions of records) as you can optimize the query execution with your data source based on your workbook needs. Also, feel free to consult your database team or experts at your company; they may be able to point you to a library of standard queries they have created.

The Multiple Tables option from the Connection dialog is quite powerful. Please **click on Multiple Tables**. The Connection dialog will change in appearance, shown below on the left. To add a new table to our data source, **click on Add New Table** and the Add Table dialog appears, shown below on the right. To add the *Returns* table to the data source**, click on *Returns*.** You also must specify a join path; this is how the two tables (*Orders* and *Returns*) will be merged together before returning the data source to you.

Using the Multiple Tables option for a data connection, the Add Table dialog is shown on the right

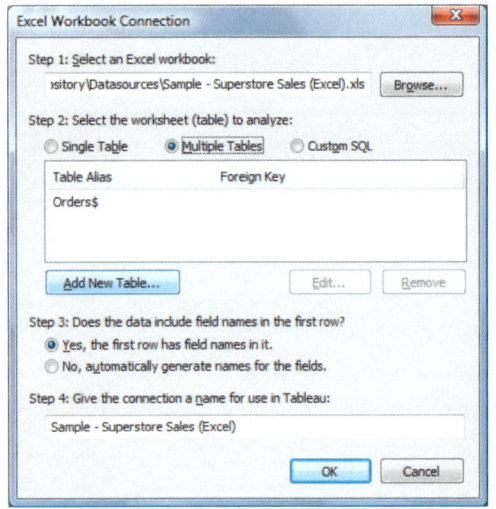
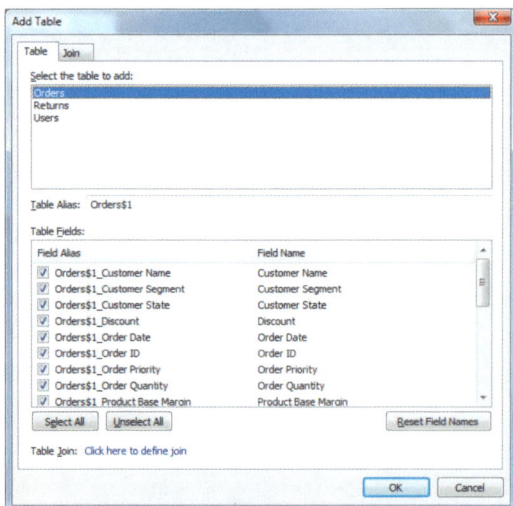

By default, Tableau will use identically named rows in the two tables to join the data. It also will default to an inner join which means only rows that exist with the same values will be returned (in other words, rows in *Orders* that don't also exist in *Returns* won't be returned via this data source.) If you wanted all rows returned in the *Orders* table and only matching rows from the *Returns* table, you would select left join instead of inner join. For this example, **select Left join and click OK** to close the Add Table dialog.

Adding *Returns* to the data source using a left join, a stacked bar chart of returns (from *Returns* table) by *Customer Segment* as a *Percent of Sales* and *Sum of Sales*

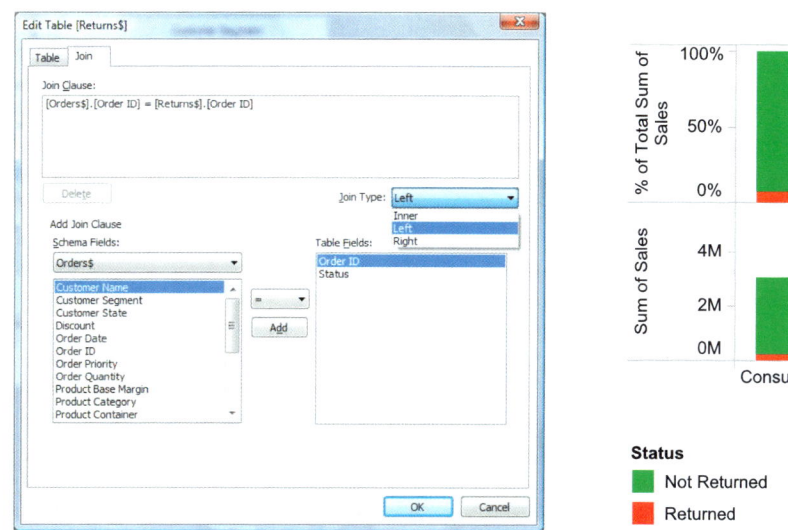
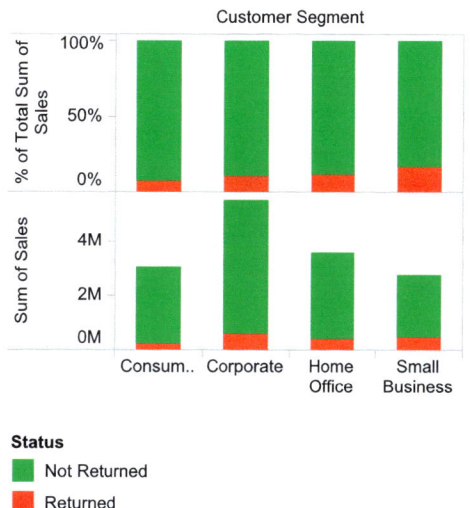

The value "Not Returned" in the stacked bar chart above has been recoded from Null or missing. All rows in *Orders* that did not have a matching Order ID row in *Returns* show the value Null in the data returned from the new multi-table query.

One final performance note related to queries. Tableau automatically queries the data source or Tableau extract every time you change the view specification (e.g., changes in marks or shelves). For very large data sources, this is not always preferred since you may want to make several changes to your view before refreshing the data and waiting for your query to complete to update the view. You can toggle the automatic updates feature on and off from **Data -> Automatic Updates or click the** 🖵 **toolbar icon.** If they are turned off, any changes made to the view specification will cause the view to be grayed out until you refresh the data via **Data -> Run Update or click the** ⟳ **toolbar icon.**

Extracts to accelerate your data exploration in Tableau

A Tableau extracts is a copy or subset of the whole data source that you can use to improve query performance, enable certain advanced capabilities and perform analysis when away from a connection to your database. You can create an extract with or without filters to include only the data that you want in the extract. Extracts allow you to analyze data stored in large data sources (often multi-table joins can take a while with many databases) that would slow down your work in Tableau.

You can start the extract process during data source creation or when using data from **Data -> Extract**. Extract sizes can be limited via multiple methods during the extract process. You can use field specific filters (e.g., Sales greater than $1,000.00), you can aggregate data for visible dimensions (significantly reducing the amount of data stored in the extract based on the current non-hidden item structure), you can roll up data based on years, quarters, months, day, hours, minutes or seconds (significantly reducing rows with transactional data), or you can take a subset of the data based on a subset of the number of records (percent or specified number of rows.) Please note that the last option is NOT the same as a random sample if your data are ordered in the data source, it is merely the initial records from the data source up to the number of rows specified.

The Extract Data dialog with filtering by *Sales* amount and data aggregation by visible dimensions and by day

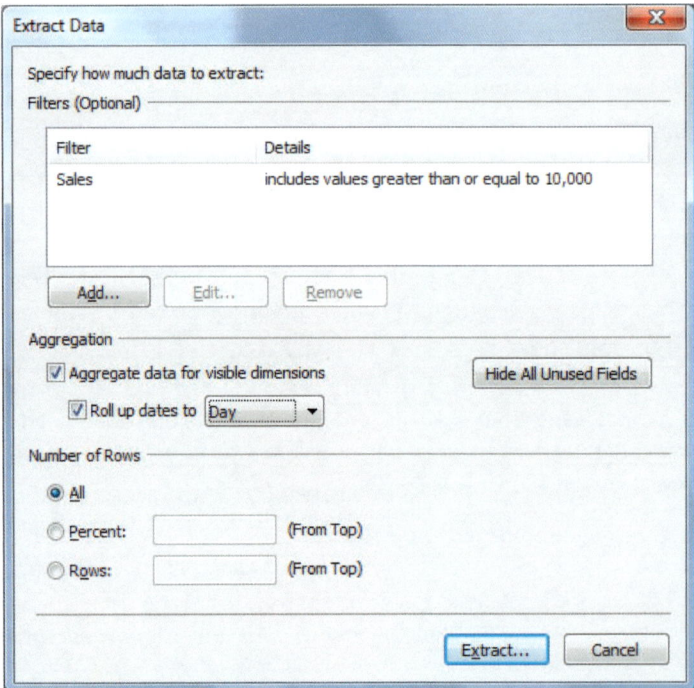

After specifying the details of the extract to create, you will need to save the extract to a local file location. Extracts cannot be saved to a network drive for performance reasons. Depending on the size and complexity of your data source and the filters specified by you, extracting data can take significant amounts of time. However, after the extract is created, you will see significantly improved response times. By default, the created extract becomes the data source for the current workbook.

You can toggle between using the extract and using the entire data source by selecting **Data > Use Extract**. You can review the extract properties by selecting **Data -> Extract Properties**, which will show you the disk size of the extract (e.g., 50 MB), the location, the date last refreshed and all applied filters, aggregations and row limits. If you want to remove an extract, select **Data -> Remove Extract**. When removing the extract from the project, you will be given the option to also delete it from your hard drive; *do not delete it unless you are certain it isn't in use by other workbooks.*

Here are some reasons to use extracts:

- When using a file-based data source such as text files, Microsoft Excel or Microsoft Access, extracts can improve performance for the entire data source or a subset.
- Extracts enable additional functionality for file-based data sources, such as the ability to count distinct rows (how many distinct customer names are in the orders table?).
- With large data sources (millions or even billions of rows), you can improve performance and reduce database loads by using extract subsets (e.g., all records for transactions over $1,000.00.) In my multiple experiences with extracts, query performance improvements of 100%-500% are typical. There are times when extracts may be slower, especially if you have a very large number of levels in multiple dimensional data items or if your database source is extremely fast.
- As an alternative to disabling automatic updates, you can create an extract with a subset of the data to enable rapid view development with very large data sources. Once you have developed the desired view, you can switch to the complete data source.

One last thought on extracts- with faster PC's and particularly the new solid-state hard drives recently available, extracts are a very powerful option for heavy users of Tableau. I would strongly recommend examining the new solid-state hard drives that can improve performance over traditional ones by a factor of 100%-300%, which means more time understanding the data and less time waiting for your queries!

Page intentionally left blank for proper book pagination.

Chapter 10

Sharing your insights from Tableau

Chapter Highlights

- Exporting Images

- Exporting Data

- Publish as PDF

- Workbooks and Packaged Workbooks

- Tableau Reader

- Tableau Server

Everyone enjoys the company of someone who shares! Now that you have created amazing graphs and gained valuable insights– you are probably eager to share your work with your managers, co-workers, friends and even your family. This chapter will cover many of the capabilities available in Tableau that you can use to distribute your work and make it the talk of the town!

Exporting images is one of the most common needs and Tableau makes it quick and painless. The data used in your view can also be exported to several formats. The ability to publish your work as a PDF is very handy for distribution because it can be opened by a widely used document reader found on the internet. Saving work done in Tableau is fast and simple with workbooks. You can also embed the data as a packaged workbook if you need to send it to an external party- they will be able to look at the data behind the pretty pictures. Tableau Reader is a free download that people can use to interact with your packaged workbooks and it includes a subset of the full Tableau product functionality.   Finally, Tableau Server is a wonderful product that can easily make Tableau available inside and outside your organization with no installation of software required- all you need is a web browser such as Internet Explorer, Firefox, Safari or Google Chrome!

Exporting Images to other applications

Since Tableau allows you to create exceptional graphs, you will likely want to export your gems to other applications such as Word, PowerPoint and other Windows applications. There are three means to export graphs from Tableau:

- Windows copy and paste
- Export as an image file
- Publish as an Adobe PDF file (this option is covered in a later section of this chapter)

For the most common uses of exporting images, creating a Microsoft Word report or PowerPoint presentation, Windows copy and paste functionality is fast and seamless. It will work well unless you require images of extremely high quality.

Copy graphs with Windows copy and paste

1. Select **Edit -> Copy -> Image** or **<Ctrl> + C.** The Copy Image dialog box appears. The elements available for selection are based on the view type you are using.

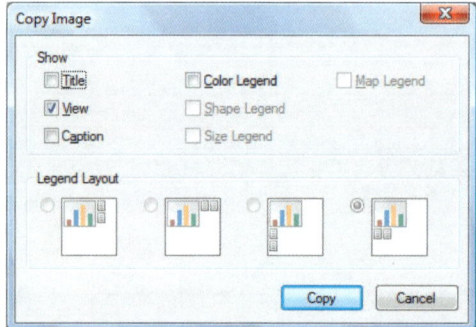

2. Under Show, **select the view elements you want to include in the image**.
3. If you wish to include a legend, **use Legend Layout to determine its location.**
4. **Click Copy**, and the selected elements will be added to the Windows clipboard.
5. To paste a standard quality image of your graph into your Word or PowerPoint document, select **Paste from the Home Menu or the Edit Menu** (depending on which version you have) **or type <Ctrl>-V** (for all versions).
6. For a higher quality graph image, select **Paste Special from the Home or Edit Menu** (depending on your version). **Choose the Picture (Enhanced Metafile) format** to paste the highest quality image into your application.

Export graphs as an image file

1. Select **File -> Export > Image**. The Export Image dialog appears, which is identical to the Copy Image dialog except the Copy button is replaced with the Save button. Once again, the elements available for selection are based on the view type you are using.
2. **Select the view elements you want to include in the image.** If you are using a legend, **choose the Legend Location. Click Save.** The Save Image file dialog appears. **Type the desired file name.**
3. Select the file type to use when saving the graph. There are four file types available.
   a. *PNG (Portable Network Graphics):* this is the best choice due to the smallest size and best resolution.
   b. *EMF (Enhanced Metafile):* next best choice, larger size than PNG with best resolution.
   c. *BMP (Windows Bitmap):* third best choice, very large size with best resolution.
   d. *JPEG Image (the default):* lower quality and moderate file size, not recommended.
4. **Click Save.** The graph image file is exported by Tableau based on your selections.

Use copied or exported Tableau images in other applications

Exporting Data to other applications and even back to Tableau

Given Tableau's broad functionality, there are few reasons to export your data from Tableau. In case you need this capability, Tableau has several ways to export the data that appears in your view. To export the detailed data *underlying your view* (in contrast to the data appearing in your view), refer back to the "View Underlying Data" section in the Chapter 8.

A few tips to consider when exporting data from Tableau:
- The fields exported are the fields that are placed on the worksheet shelves. However, data items on the Filters shelf are excluded unless you also use them on another shelf.
- To include fields without placing them on the Rows, Columns or Marks shelves, **place them on the Level of Detail shelf.**
- You can select all of the data view to export by **Edit -> Select All**, or any portion of the data view by **using the <Ctrl> key and clicking on items or by clicking and dragging.** One exception is copying or exporting to a cross-tab, which always uses all the data in the view.

To follow the examples of exports, follow these steps to create this view:
1. **Open the "Sample - Coffee Chain (Access)" data source.**
2. **Click on *Area Code* and *Profit*, select Show Me! Accept the default view choice by clicking OK.**
3. **Add *Market* to the Color shelf.**

Sample view to use with export examples

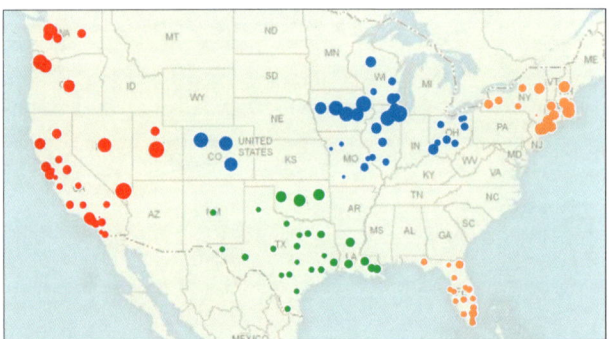

Copy records to clipboard

This method is useful for pasting records into another application such as Excel or Notepad. You must select part or all of the view to use this method. **Drag over the points in Washington and Oregon to highlight them, and then Edit -> Copy -> Data or <Ctrl> + C**. The records are now available for pasting into another application. Here is what Tableau copies to the clipboard:

Area Code	Market	Latitude (generated)	Longitude (generated)	Sum of Profit
206	West	47.56750603	-122.2772318	$3,823
253	West	47.20133964	-122.4239439	$2,040
360	West	47.03877522	-121.4635792	$1,829
425	West	47.51552986	-121.9352075	$2,017
503	West	45.45323003	-123.2324076	$5,009
509	West	47.34337024	-119.0153828	$1,696
541	West	43.82340572	-120.2964004	$3,378
971	West	45.20118729	-122.7083396	$4,052

Export records to Microsoft Access

This method is useful for large data volumes (greater than 50,000 records) or using the data in Microsoft Access. With Washington and Oregon highlighted, **go to File -> Export -> Data**. The Export Data to Access dialog appears. **Type a name for the new Access database file or select an existing Access database file**. **Click Save**. The second Export Data to Access dialog appears, as shown below. Note that you can name the table for use in Access, connect to this export after it is created and select whether the entire view or just the selected parts of the view data are exported. **Click OK** to complete the export. If you keep the defaults, the data exported is identical to that found in the above table.

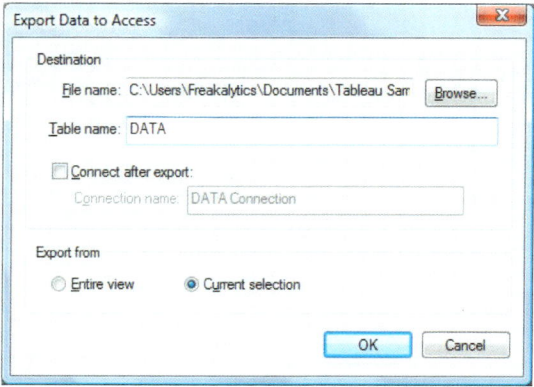

Copy or Export cross-tab to clipboard

In the two previous sections, when you copied records from a clipboard and exported records to Access, the data records exported were based on your view selection. These two methods, copying and exporting cross-tabs to clipboards, ignore your selections of marks in the view during export. Also, they both format your export in a simplified version of cross-tabs, but the export method has more attractive formatting.

To follow the next two examples, **add *Product Type* to the Level of Detail below the *Area Code* item** (this information will appear in the view when you hover over a data point). To copy the view data to a cross-tab format, **click on Edit -> Copy -> Cross-tab**. The data are now available for pasting into another application, in a format similar to this:

Market	Area Code	Product Type Coffee	Product Type Espresso	Product Type Herbal Tea	Product Type Tea
Central	216	$74	$473	$28	$67
Central	217	$672	$682	$68	$319
Central	224	$225	$455	$405	
Central	234	$240	$426	$61	$511

The exported table actually has 156 rows, but the table above shows just the first 4 rows for brevity. This simple cross-tab format is good for use with other applications beyond Excel.

To export this view as a cross-tab to Excel, **click File -> Export -> Cross-tab to Excel**. Note that using this method will automatically open Excel, create a new workbook and place the cross-tab export in an Excel worksheet. This method is slower than the copy and paste method. Also, this method does not connect Excel to the data source used in Tableau nor does it place the data in a Pivot Table. An example of the formatting created by this method:

Market	Area Code	Product Type			
		Coffee	Espresso	Herbal Tea	Tea
Central	216	74	473	28	67
	217	672	682	68	319
	224	225	455	405	
	234	240	426	61	511
	262	765	540	960	334
	303	1712	1212	544	459
	309	539	1081	560	389

Again, for brevity, this table has been truncated. Compared to the copy function, the column headers for "Product Type" and the row headers for "Market" are not repeated for each product type or record, respectively, making the table easier to read.

It is important to note that the Export Cross-tab to Excel method has much better formatting of the view in Excel than the Copy method. For example, you have to adjust column-widths with the copy method, but the Export method does not require any adjustment and results in a very attractive cross-tab.

Publish as PDF- export your views to Adobe Acrobat format

The Adobe Acrobat Reader and PDF files are ubiquitous in the PC and Mac worlds. It is only natural that Tableau would use the PDF format as a way to distribute insights created in Tableau.

To publish to a PDF file from Tableau:

1. Specify page setup options for each sheet in your workbook, **File -> Page Setup**
    a. Key page setup options include
        i. What parts of the view to display
        ii. Show all pages based on the items placed on the Pages shelf (the default is to only show the current page at time of printing)
        iii. Legend layout
        iv. Page margins and centering
        v. Page scaling, e.g., you can fit to 1 pages wide by 2 pages tall
        vi. View title and captions
2. **Select File -> Publish as PDF** and the Publish as PDF dialog appears

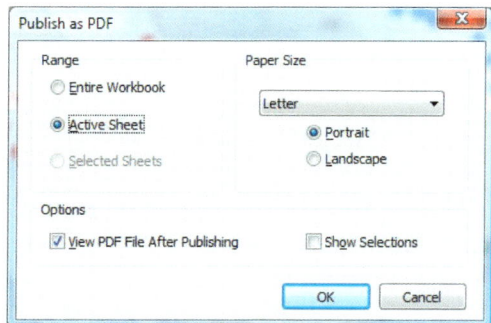

    a. Print Range
        i. Entire Workbook - includes all the sheets in the workbook
        ii. Active Sheet - includes only the sheet currently displayed
    b. Paper size
        i. If you select "Unspecified", the paper size will expand to the necessary size to fit the entire view on a single page
        ii. Other options are based on Windows standard page sizes
    c. Options
        i. Select "View PDF File After Publishing" if you want to automatically open the PDF when you are done publishing.
        ii. Clicking on Show Selections will highlight selected data points in the PDF
3. **Click OK**, the Save PDF dialog appears.
4. **Choose the location and file name and click Save.**

<u>*Packaged Workbooks- take Tableau on the road!*</u>

The vast majority of Tableau workbooks use external data sources. Workbooks can reference file-based data sources such as Excel, Access, text file and even Tableau Extracts. By default, when you save a Tableau workbook, the *connection* information to the data sources is saved in the workbook (but not the data source itself). This means that the next time you open the workbook, the views are updated with any changes made to the external data and any background images you may have used.

In general, saving the workbook with just the connection information is a good route to follow. However, if you need to use the workbook while away from the data source or send it to someone at another organization with no access to your data source, you can include the data source and the background images in a special workbook type - the packaged workbook.

Tableau packaged workbooks contain the workbook, copies of any local data sources and any background images. Saving the workbook as a packaged workbook also loses any references to the original data sources and images, instead replacing all of these connections with the packaged sources. Note that the only items included in the packaged workbook are local file based sources, such as Excel, Access, text files, Tableau Data Extracts and local database cube files. If you are using a remote database connection, such as Oracle, SQL Server or DB2, you must create a Tableau Extract in order to include these data sources in the packaged workbook.

To save your workbook as a packaged workbook, **click File -> Save As** and the Save As dialog appears. **Change the Save as type: dropdown to Tableau Packaged Workbook (*.twbx)**. One big drawback of this approach is that the data size of the actual workbook can grow very large! This is dependent on the size of the data sources being packaged with the workbook.   While Tableau uses data compression to minimize the overall size of the packaged workbook, size could still be a problem with data source sizes in the millions of records or larger.

Packaged workbooks are saved with a different Windows file extension than the standard workbook (.twb versus .twbx). If you give this file to someone else with your current release of Tableau, or a later release, they should be able to open and interact with the packaged workbook. One important note: if you share packaged workbooks that contain Microsoft Excel 2007 or Microsoft Access 2007 data sources, you must have Microsoft Excel 2007, Microsoft Access 2007 or the Office 2007 Data Connectivity Components installed on their PC. If you do not have Office 2007, you can download the data connectivity components from the Tableau web site.

One final technical note! Packaged Workbooks can be unpackaged (much like unzipping a zipped file) at anytime from Windows Explorer. You can unpackage a workbook by **right-clicking on the packaged workbook file in Windows Explorer and selecting Unpackage**. Once unpackaging is complete, you will see the regular workbook file (.twb) and a folder containing the data sources and images from the packaged workbook.

Tableau Reader- share with your colleagues, friends and family

Tableau Reader goes beyond PDF publishing to allow anyone to view and explore your workbooks. Tableau Reader, much like Adobe Acrobat Reader, is a free product that anyone can install in just a few minutes. The application looks and behaves like the full-featured Tableau product- only the number of features has been limited.

Tableau Reader offers some great capabilities:

1. View and print workbooks or specific sheets, including annotations.
2. Dynamic interaction with workbooks including:
    a. Sorting.
    b. Filtering.
    c. Drilling up and down to change the level of detail in a view.
    d. Rapidly paging through massive amounts of data views.
3. Tableau Reader users can copy and export graphics, cross-tabs and data for use in other applications.
4. Interact with view and select outlier data points of interest for detailed viewing or export to other applications.

Tableau Reader- freely available, including many of the great Tableau features!

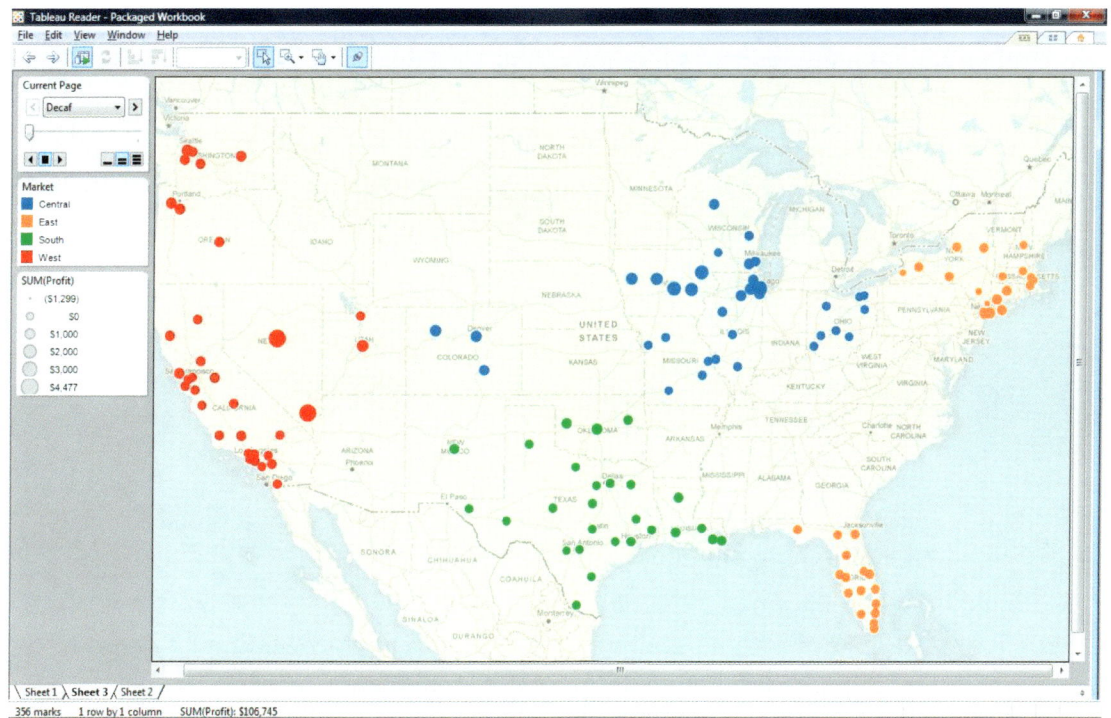

Tableau Server- powerful insights for everyone!

Tableau Server is a powerful extension of the Tableau Desktop product covered in this book. From a web browser, you can use much of the desktop functionality of Tableau across a wide community of users who want to leverage the power of Tableau from the web. Absolutely no installation of software is required and the content can be readily embedded in leading portals such as Microsoft SharePoint! Tableau Server is ideal for the casual user who frequently relies on their subject matter experts for rapid insights and guidance!

Among the many capabilities of Tableau Server:

1. Sharing your interactive workbooks created with Tableau Desktop
    a. Anyone with a browser can easily use your work. Supported browsers include Internet Explorer, Mozilla Firefox, Google Chrome and Apple Safari!
    b. Users can leverage up-to-date data with every view.
    c. Seamlessly embed Tableau views into other web applications.
    d. Publish once with server dynamic data filters data based on user permissions. This is very valuable when you have sensitive data that needs to be limited.
    e. Sort views, and keep or exclude individual data values in your view.
    f. Explore the detailed data beneath the view and export data and images.
    g. Follow links through a guided analysis path to tell a rich story.
2. Collaborate across the team
    a. All users can add explanatory notes, pose questions and suggested answers or simply contribute an opinion.
    b. Review comments to see the discussion around the data.
    c. Publish elegant dashboards to the web.
    d. Leverage powerful tags to organize information in multiple ways.
3. Browse the available views
    a. Quickly identify interesting views by browsing thumbnail images instead of only long-lists of workbook names.
    b. Sort and filter lists of available views to quickly find what you are interested in at the moment.
    c. Powerful content search finds precise and related matches. This includes the ability to search the data structure of the views. For example, you could easily find all views that use "Net Profit" in their execution!
4. Embed
    a. Truly simple embedding of Tableau views in nearly any web app using just a standard web link (URL). This method easily provides selected levels of security while widely distributing your analytic information.

Appendix - Timesaving Tips

Stephen's list of valuable keyboard shortcuts

<Ctrl> + A	Select all data in view
<Ctrl> + C	Copy selected data
<Ctrl> + D	Connect to data source
<Ctrl> + E	Describe Sheet
<Ctrl> + F	Makes the find command in the Data window active
<Ctrl> + H	Switch in and out of Presentation Mode
<Ctrl> + M	New worksheet
<Ctrl> + N	New workbook
<Ctrl> + O	Open file
<Ctrl> + P	Print
<Ctrl> + S	Save file (typically the workbook)
<Ctrl> + V	Paste clipboard
<Ctrl> + W	Swap rows and columns
<Ctrl> + X	Cut selection
<Ctrl> + Y	Redo undone action
<Ctrl> + Z	Undo last action, can be used repeatedly
<Ctrl> + (←)	Narrow view rows
<Ctrl> + (→)	Widen view rows
<Ctrl> + (↓)	Shorten view columns
<Ctrl> + (↑)	Lengthen view columns
<Ctrl> + 1	Show Me! Dialog
ENTER	Add last selected data item to the worksheet
F1	Help
<Ctrl> + F4	Delete the current worksheet or hide it if used in a dashboard
<Alt> + F4	Closes the current workbook
F4	Page forward playback- starts and stops playback of pages shelf
F5	Refresh the data source
<Ctrl> + .	Page forward one page- skip forward one page based on pages shelf
<Ctrl> + ,	Page backward one page- skip back one page based on pages shelf
<Ctrl> + Tab	Cycle through the worksheets in the open workbook
<Shift> + F6	Select mode- selects objects in view
<Shift> + F7	Pan mode- mouse pointer plus dragging moves elements in view
<Shift> + F9	Zoom mode- mouse pointer plus dragging zooms in view
F9	Run query for current view definition
F10	Toggles Automatic Updates on and off- very useful for large data sources
F12	Reverts workbook to last saved version

Standard Toolbar navigation shortcuts

The Select Tool Icon

Click on this icon (highlighted in light blue) to perform the following actions in the view:

\<Click\>	Selects an individual mark w/o retaining prior selection(s)
\<Drag\>	Selects a group of marks w/o keeping prior selection(s)
\<Ctrl\> + \<Click\>	Adds or removes individual marks to the prior selection(s)
\<Ctrl\> + \<Drag\>	Adds a group of marks to the prior selection(s)
\<Shift\> + \<Click\>	Adds individual marks to the prior selection(s) (only adds)
\<Shift\> + \<Drag\>	Adds a group of marks to the selection(s)
\<Alt\> + \<Click\>	Centers and zooms in, only shows nearby data
\<Alt\> + \<Drag\>	Focuses on the selected area
\<Alt\> + \<Shift\> + \<Drag\>	"Grabs" the view and allows panning/moving

The Zoom Tool Icon

Click on this icon (highlighted in light blue) to perform the following actions in the view:

\<Click\>	Centers and focuses on the point you clicked
\<Drag\>	Focuses on the selected area
\<Shift\> + \<Drag\>	"Grabs" the view and allows panning/moving
\<Alt\> + \<Click\>	Centers and zooms in, only shows nearby data
\<Alt\> + \<Ctrl\> + \<Click\>	Centers and zooms out from the point you clicked

The Pan Tool Icon

Click on this icon (highlighted in light blue) to perform the following actions in the view:

\<Drag\>	"Grabs" the view and allows panning/moving
\<Alt\> + \<Drag\>	Pan/move across multiple panes in a large view

Made in the USA
Lexington, KY
06 September 2010